PICTURE BOOK OF
BIRDS

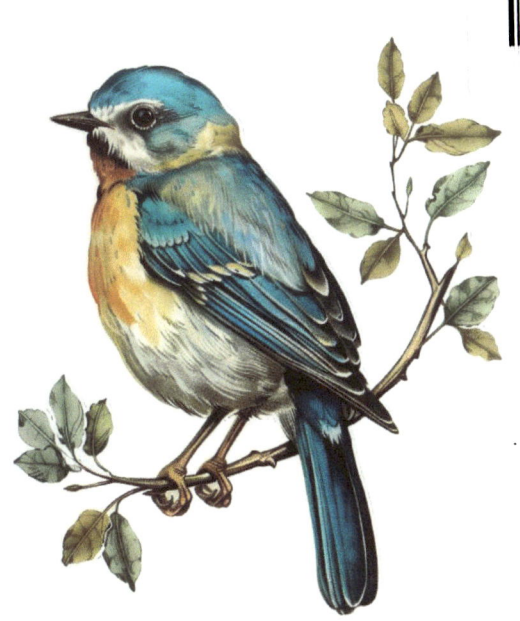

...By...

Ella Caldwell

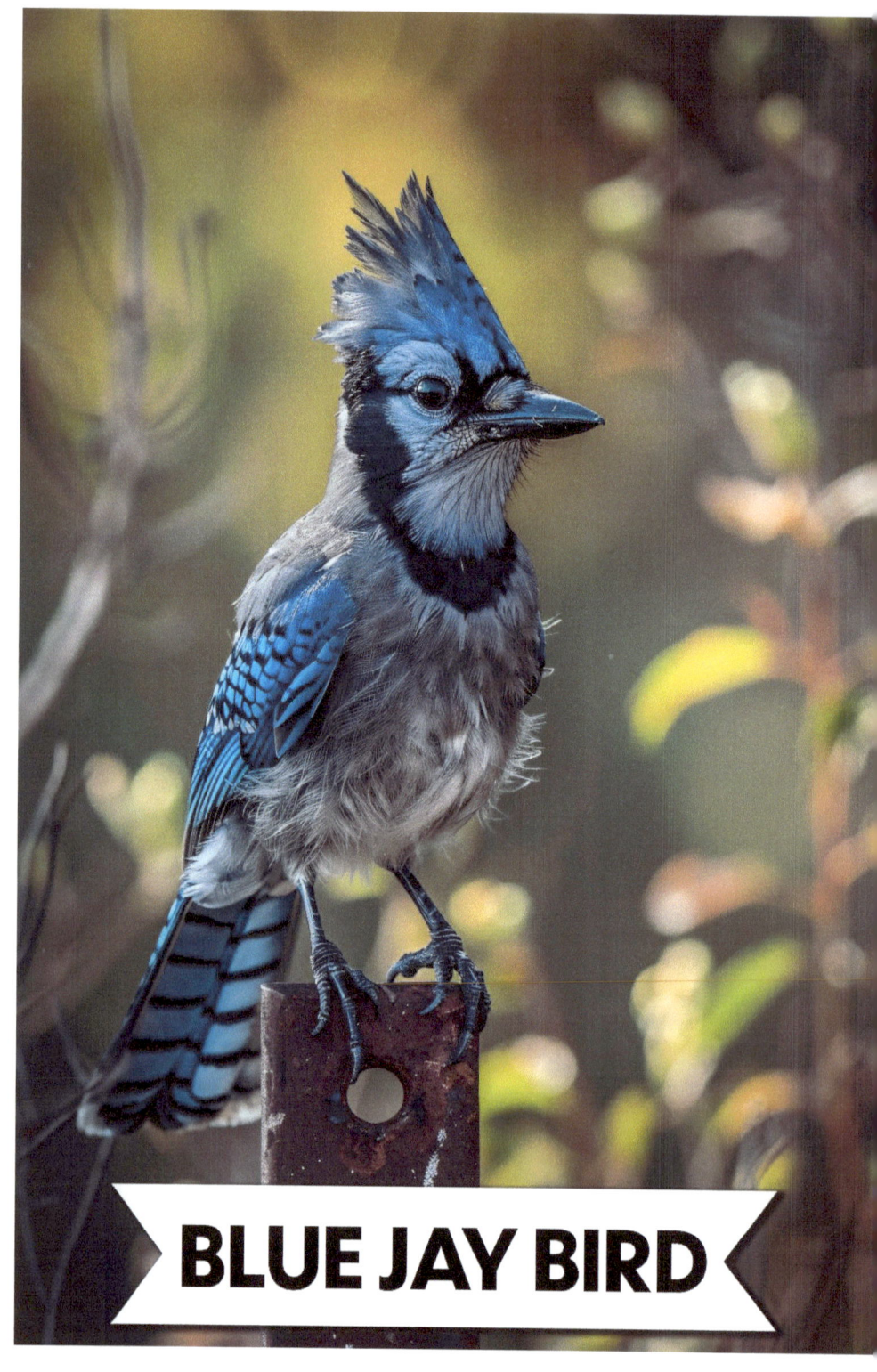

BLUE JAY BIRD

CROSSBILL

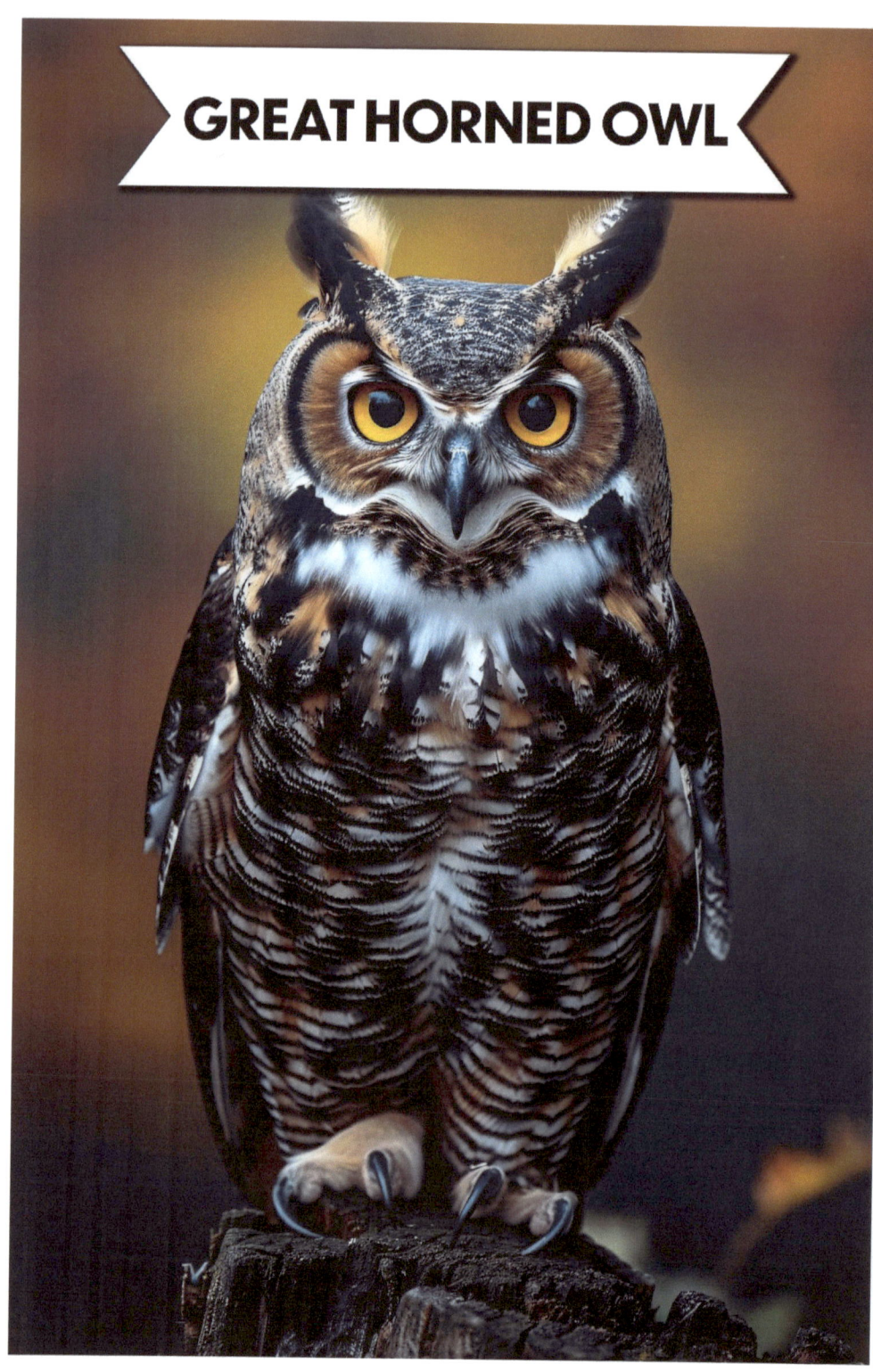

GREAT HORNED OWL

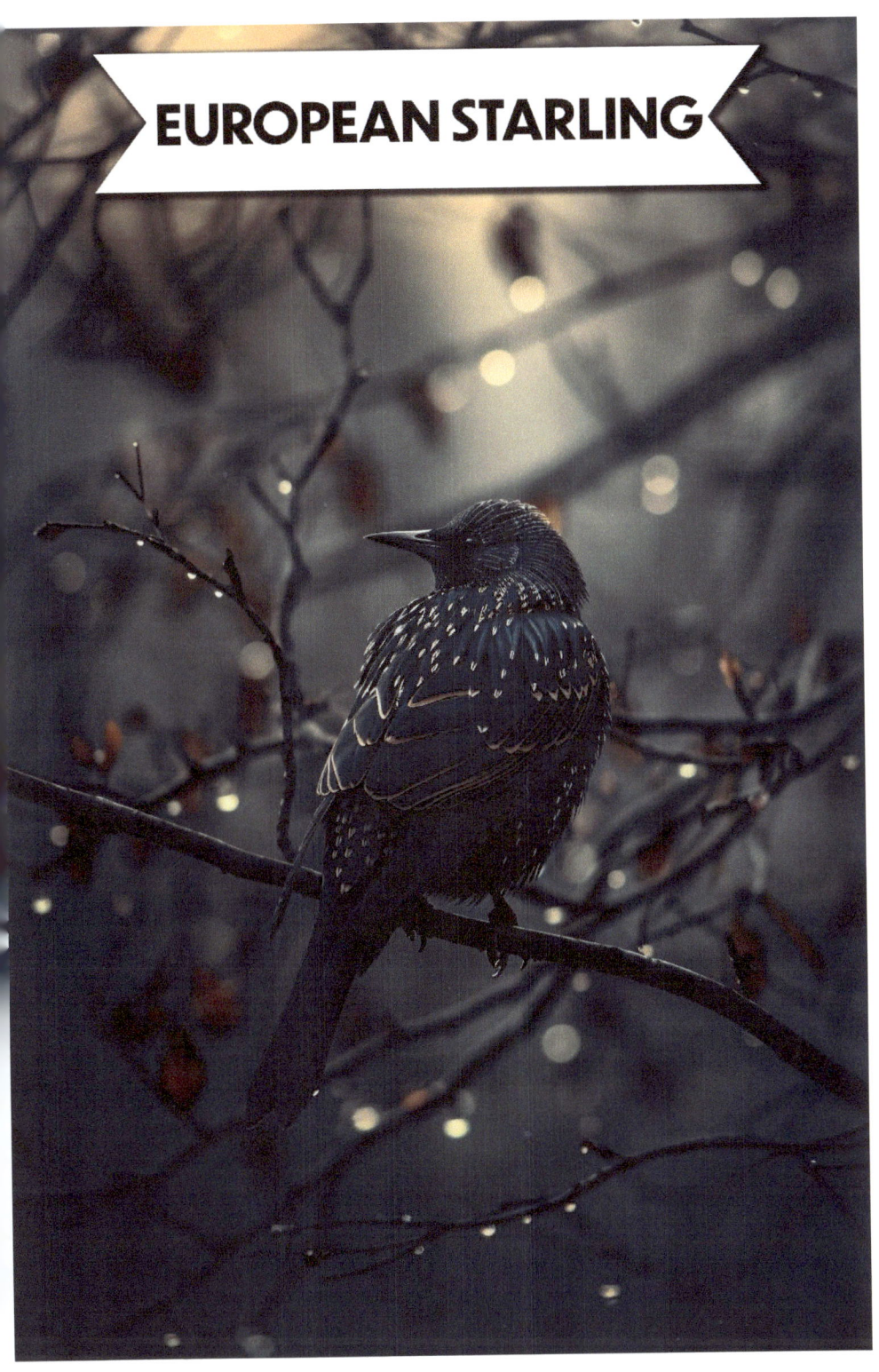

EUROPEAN STARLING

EASTERN MEADOWLARK

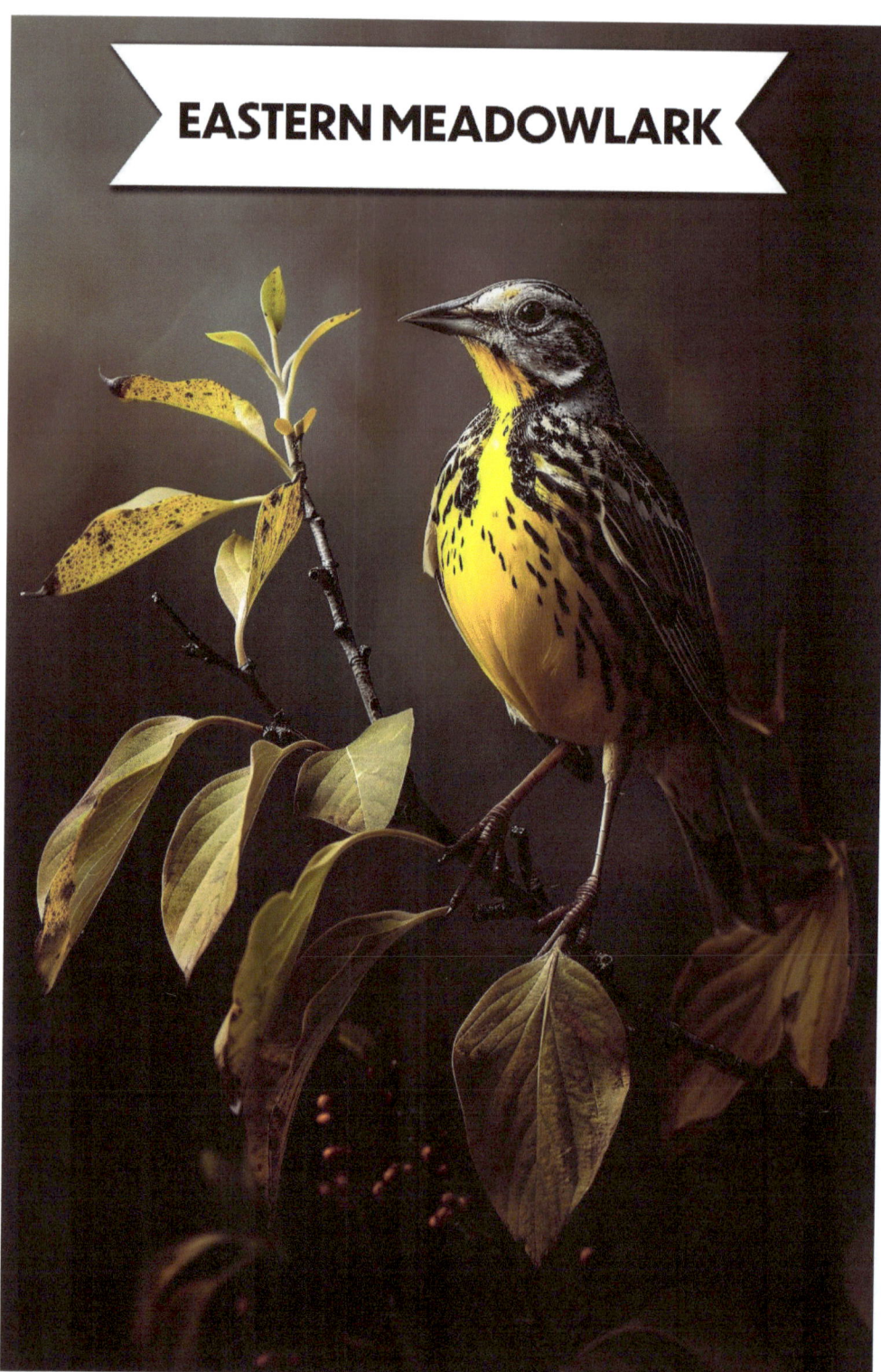

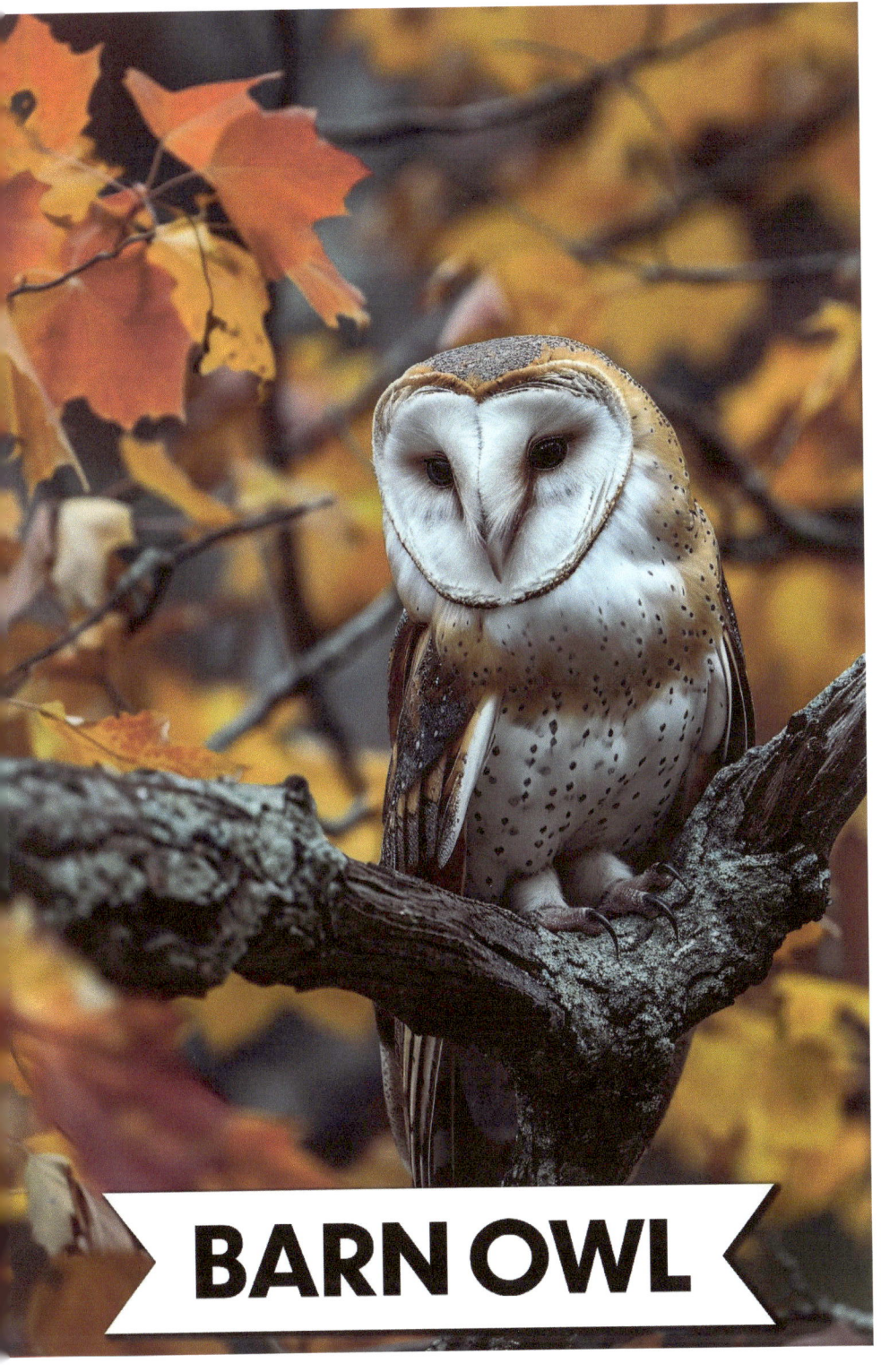

BARN OWL

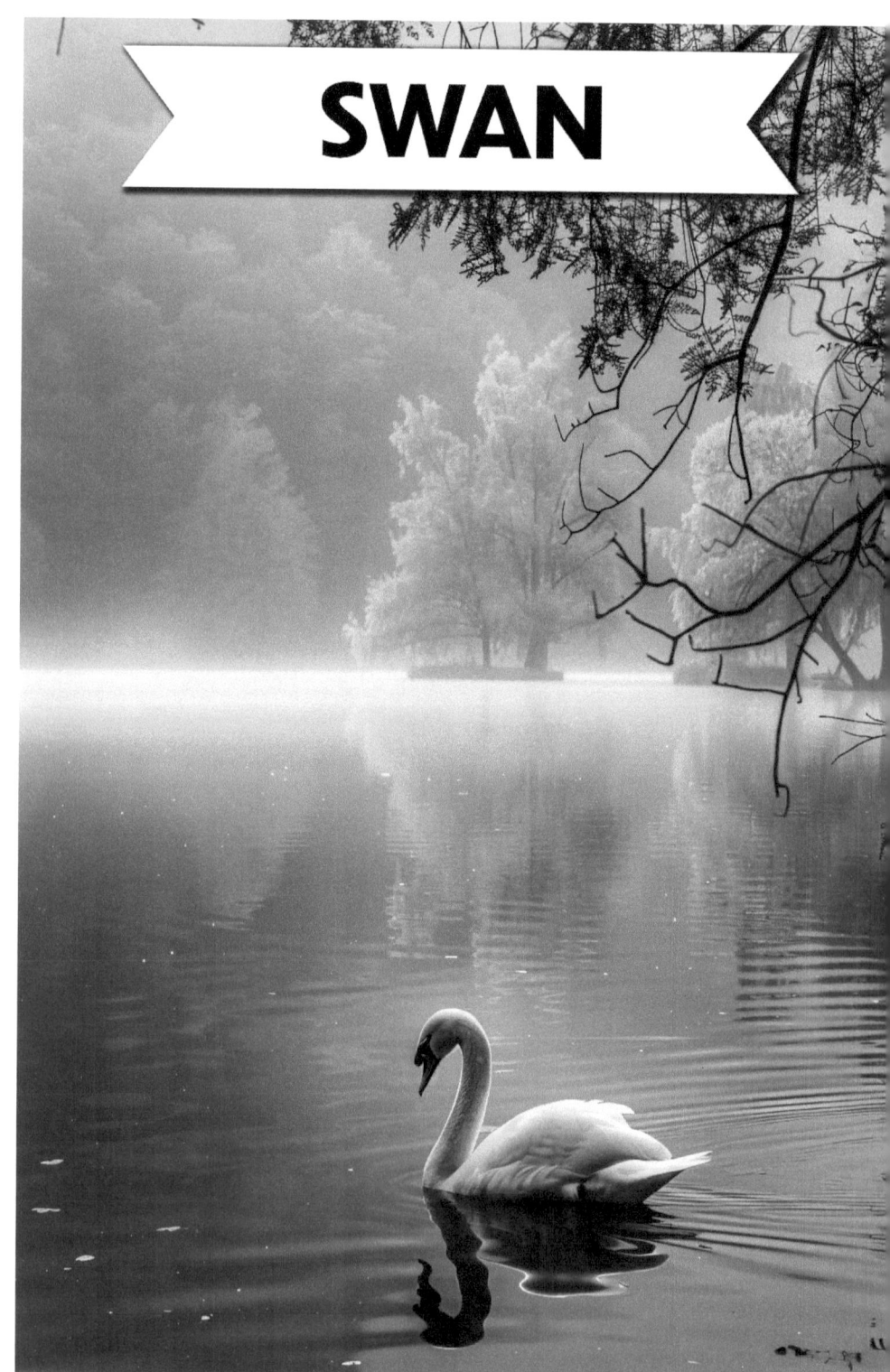

SWAN

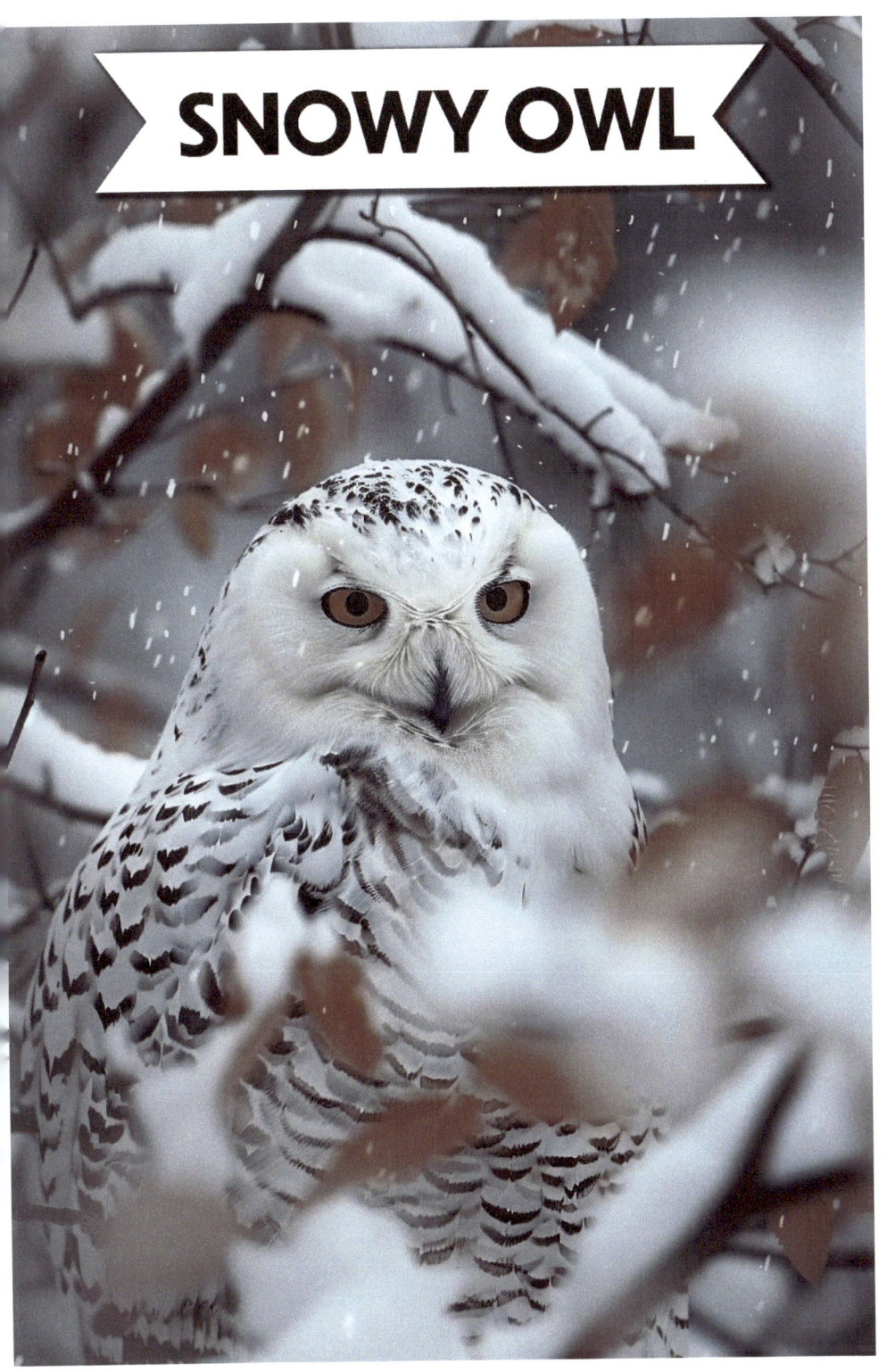

SNOWY OWL

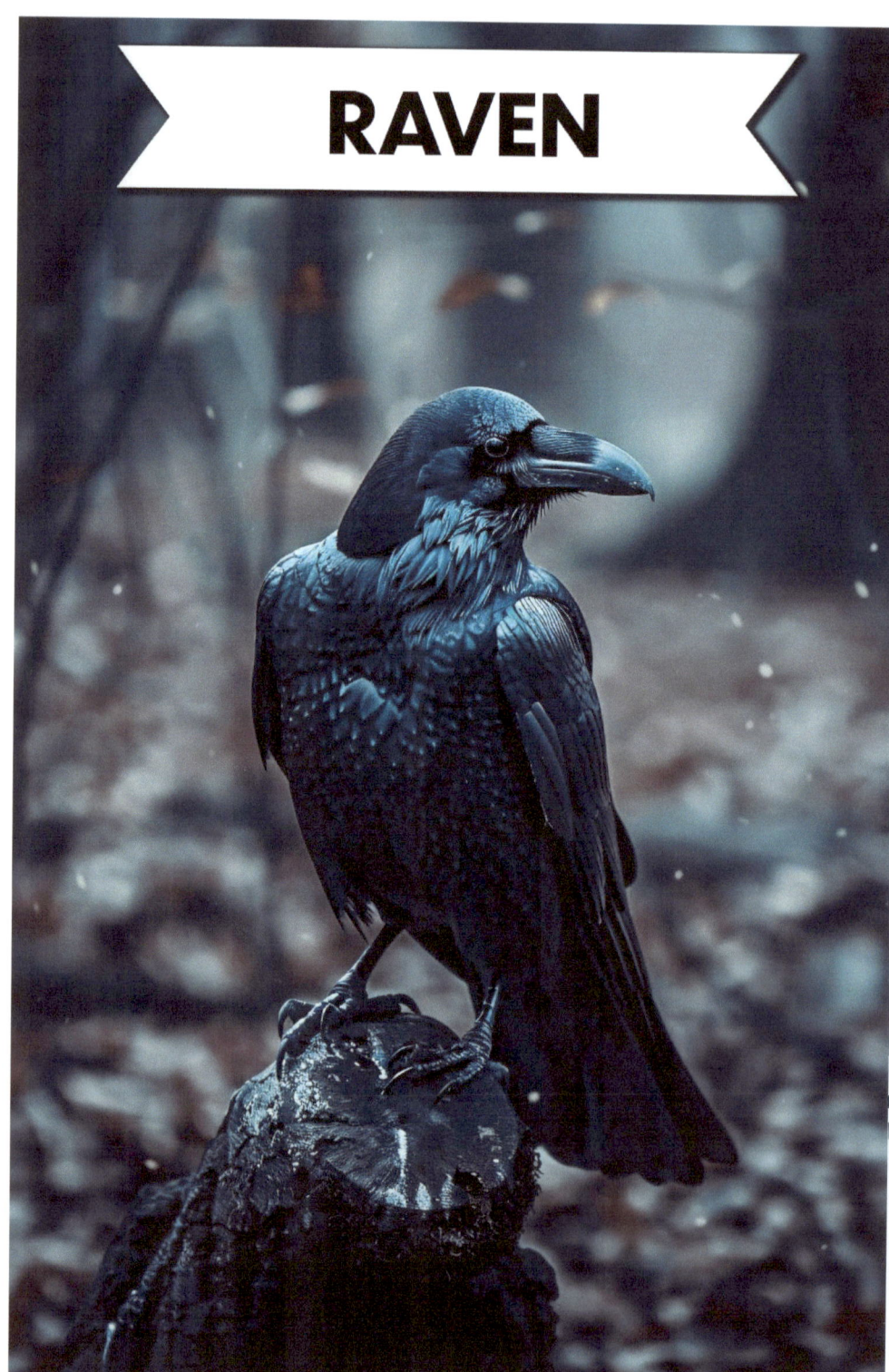

RAVEN

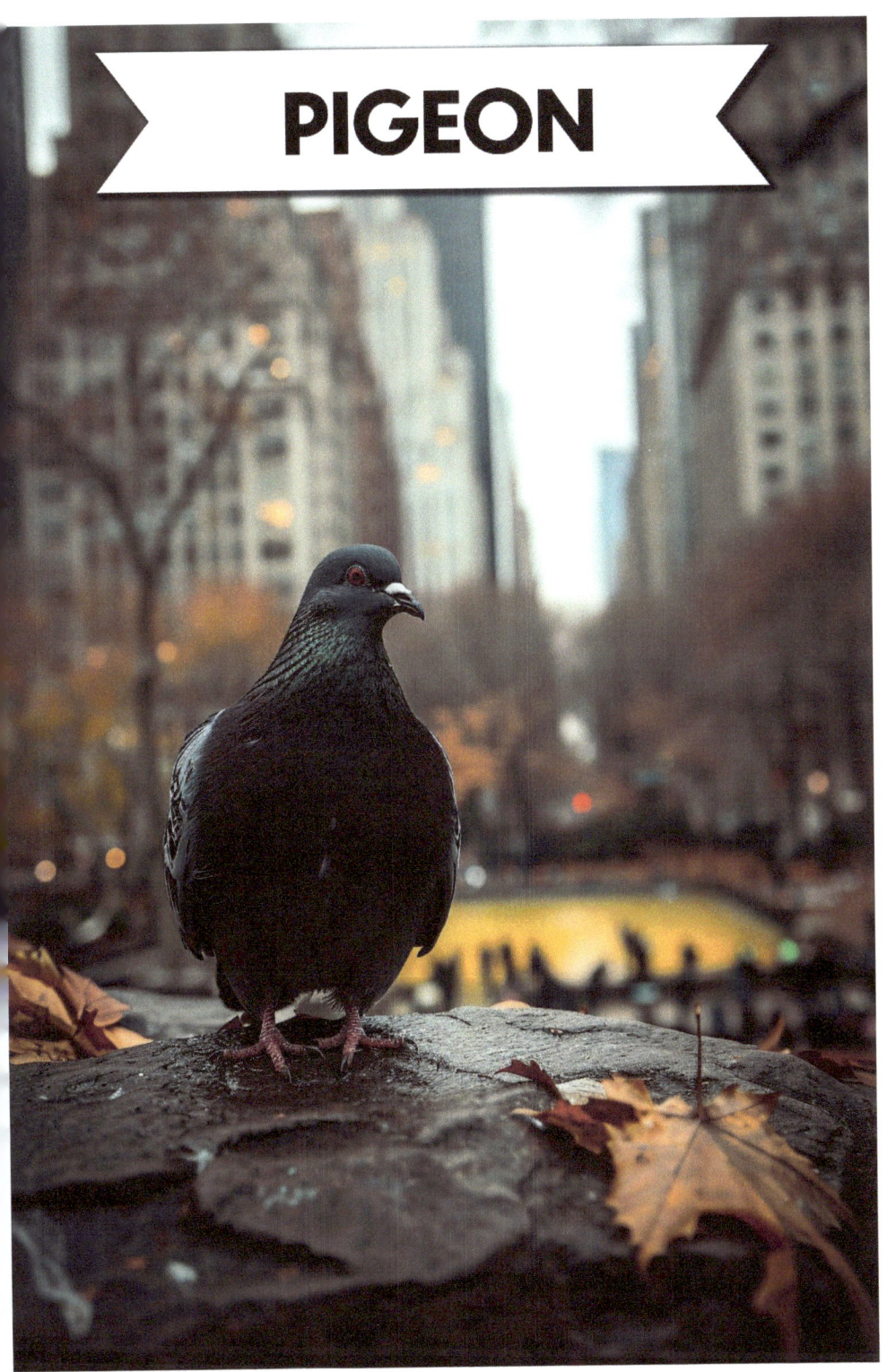

PIGEON

PEACOCK

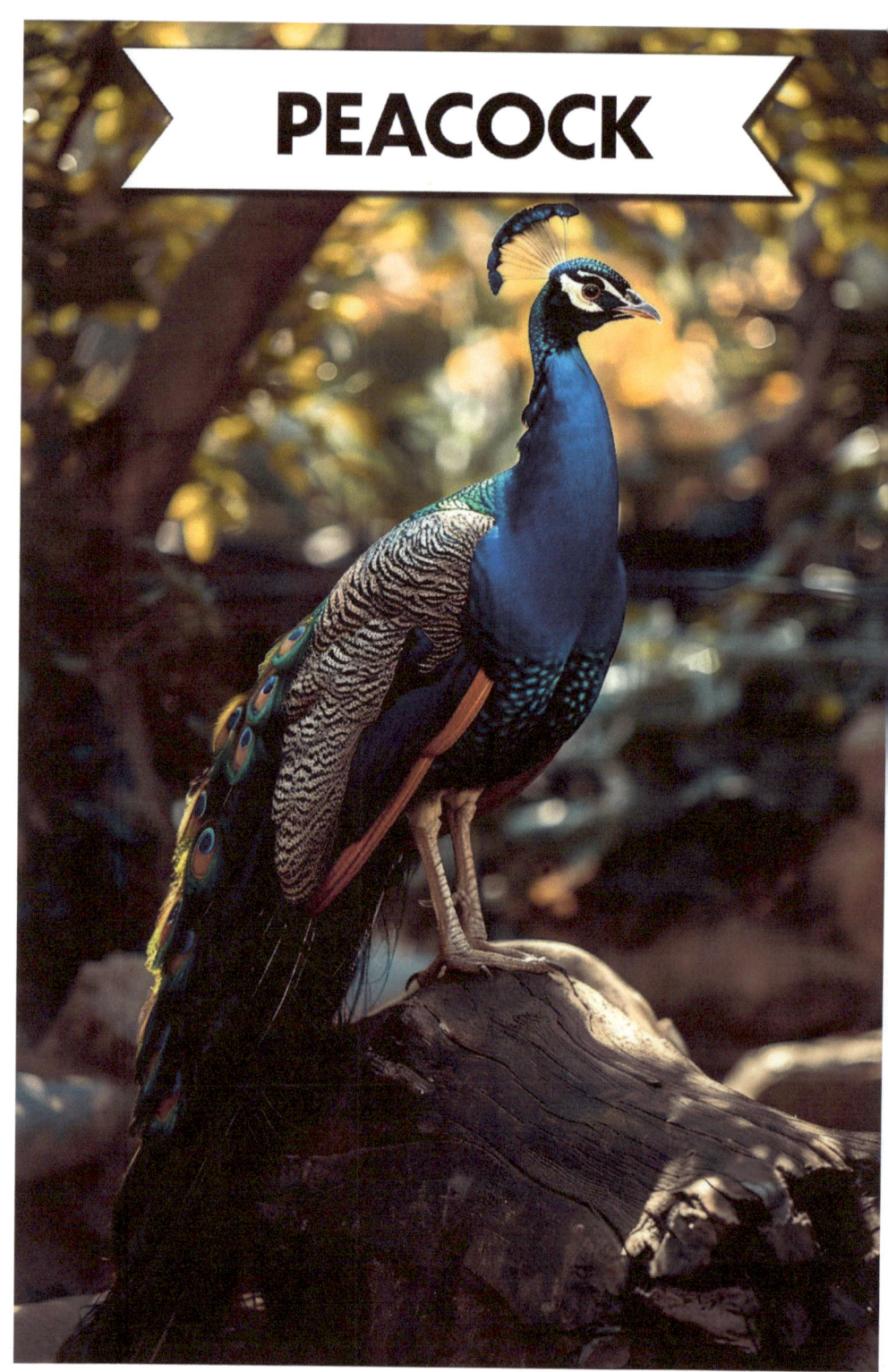

HUMMINGBIRD

FLAMINGO

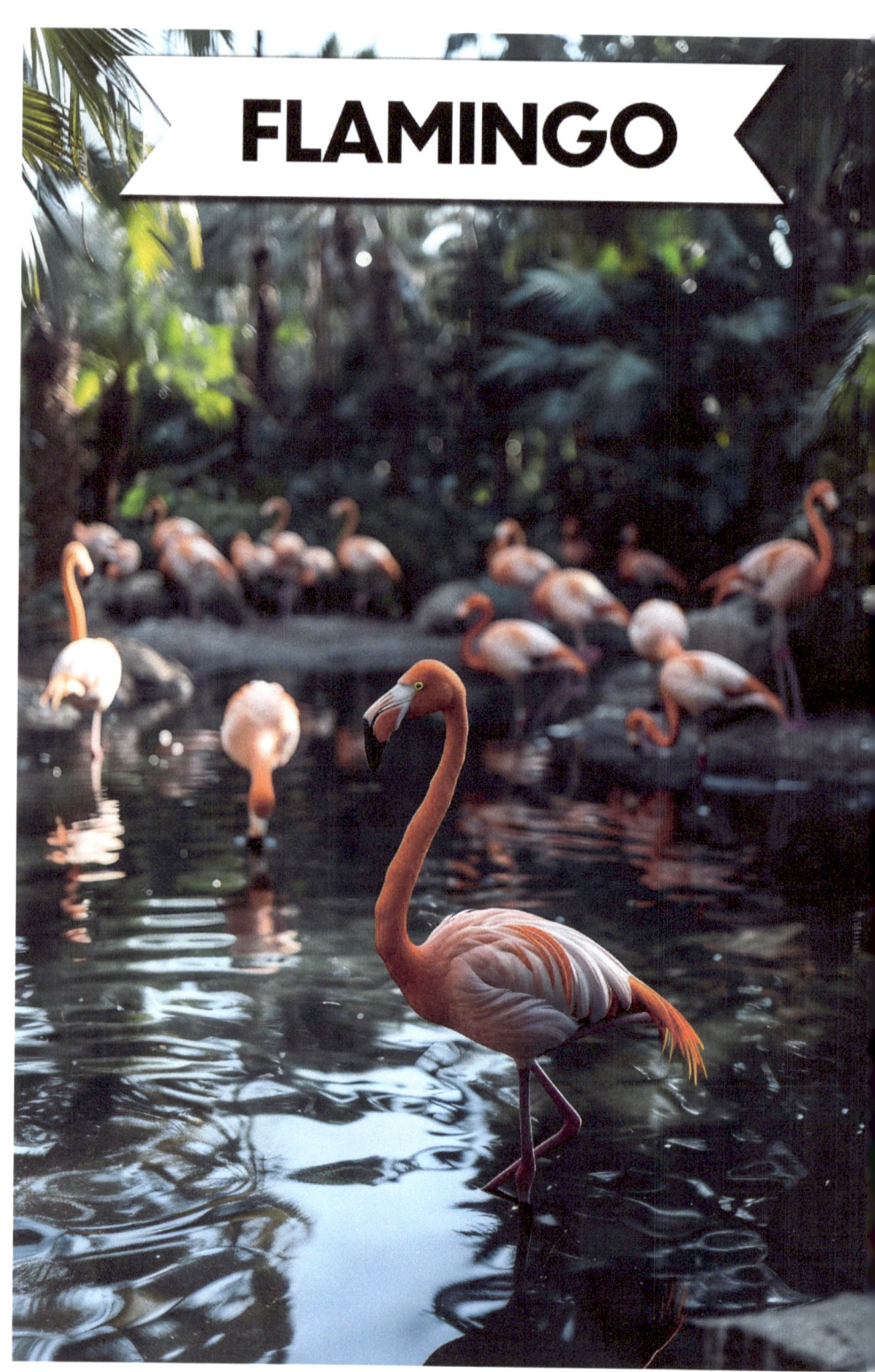

FINCH

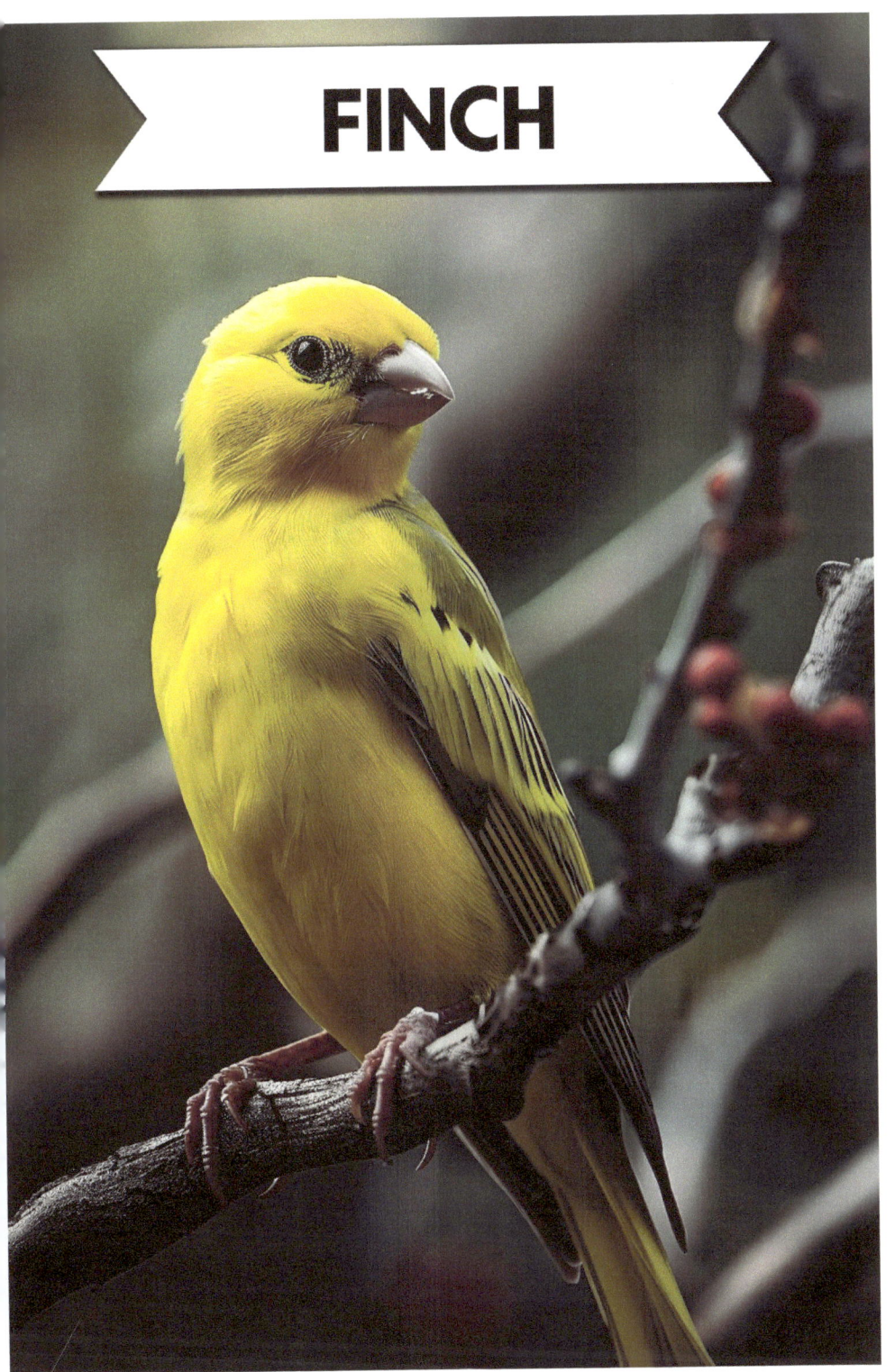

FALCON

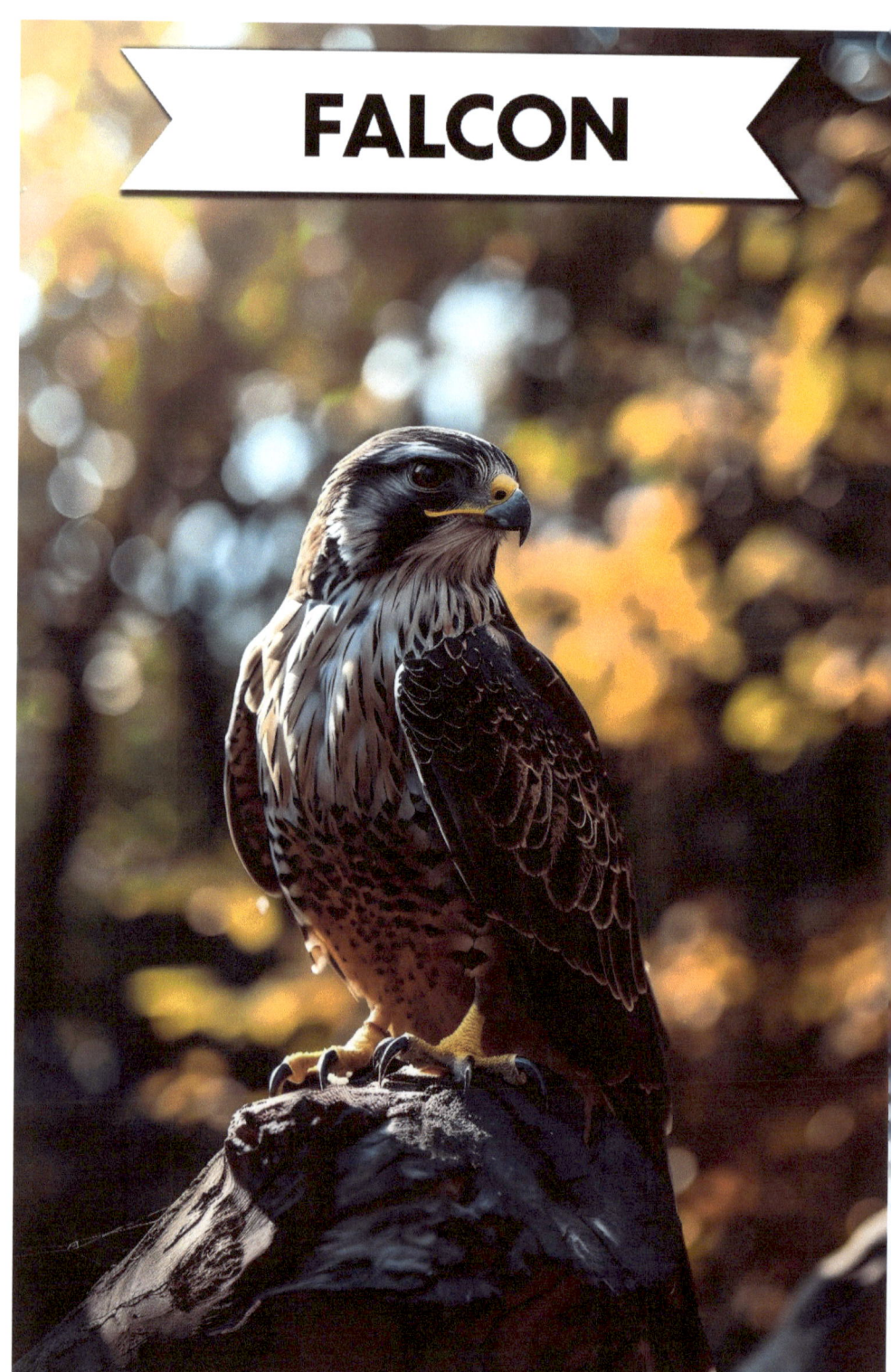

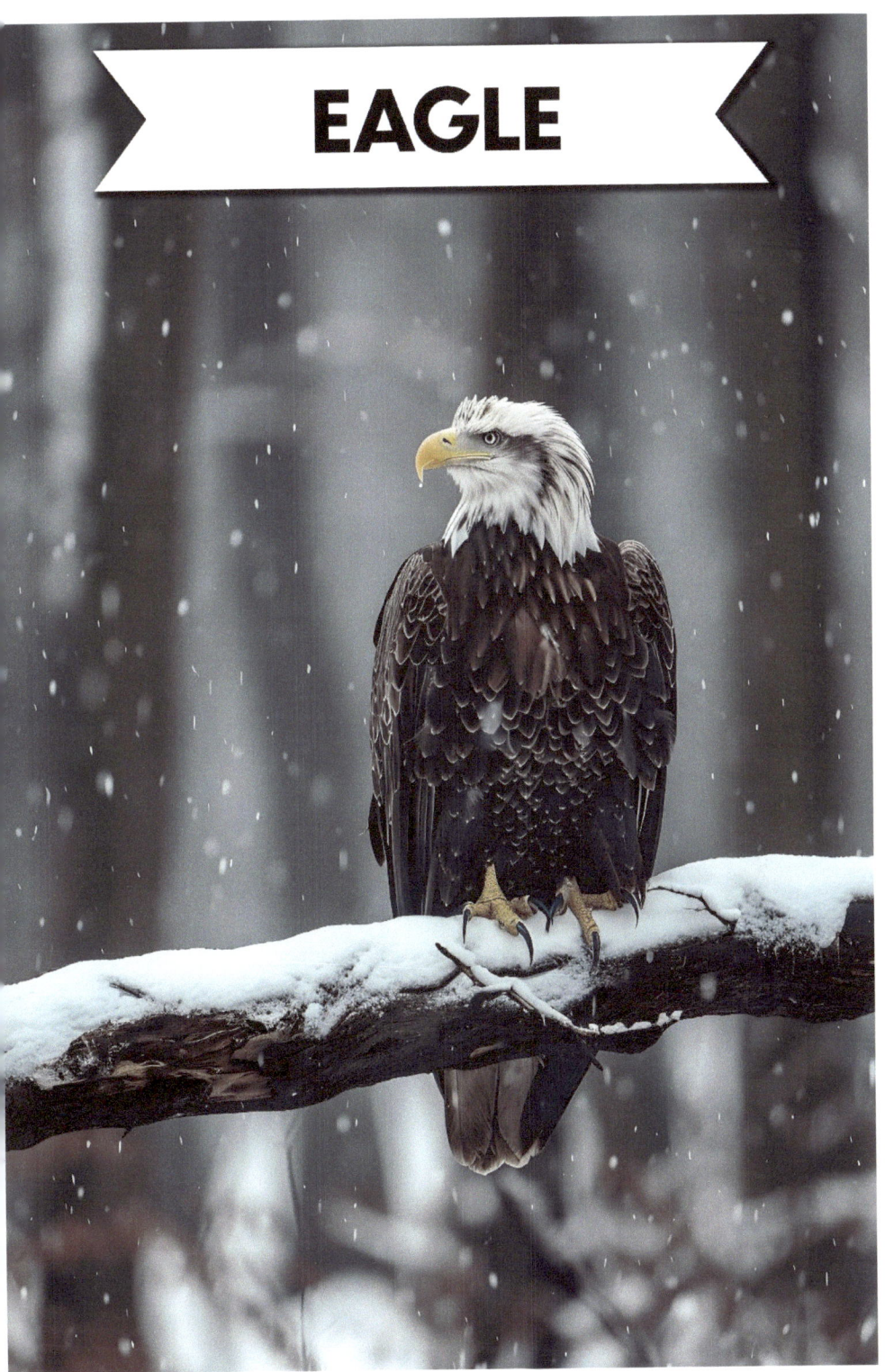

EAGLE

DUCK

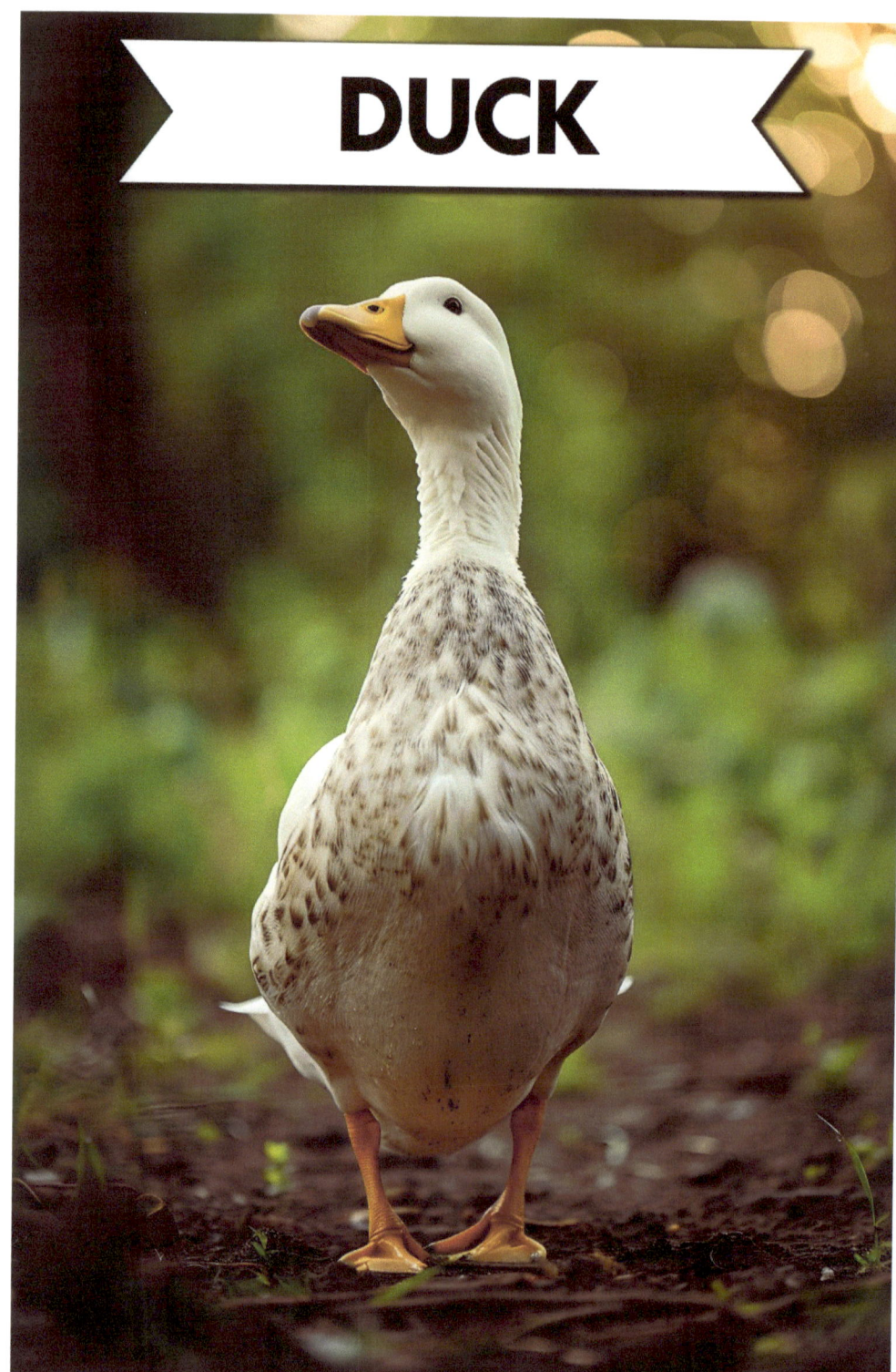

CROW

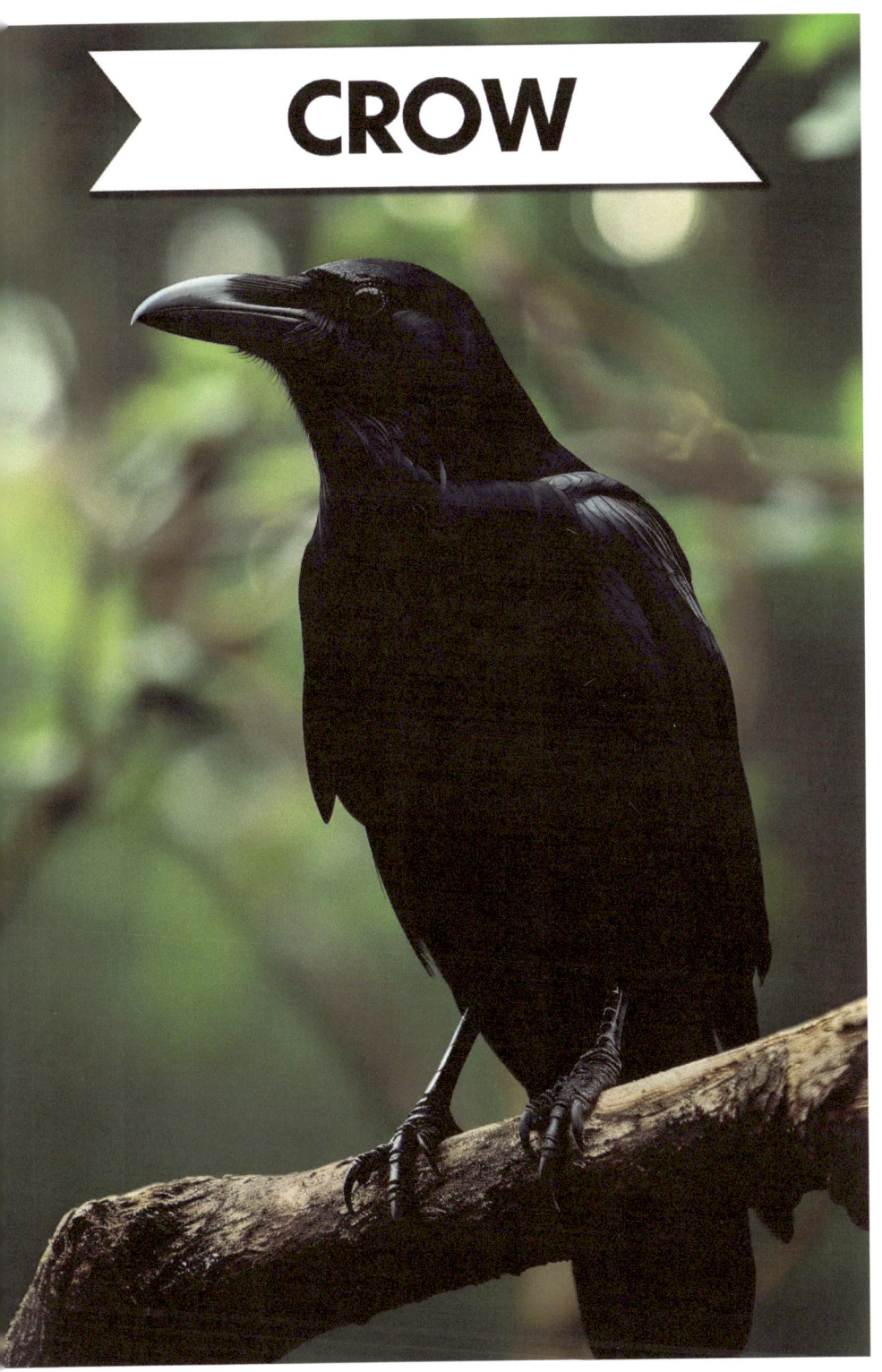

PENGUIN

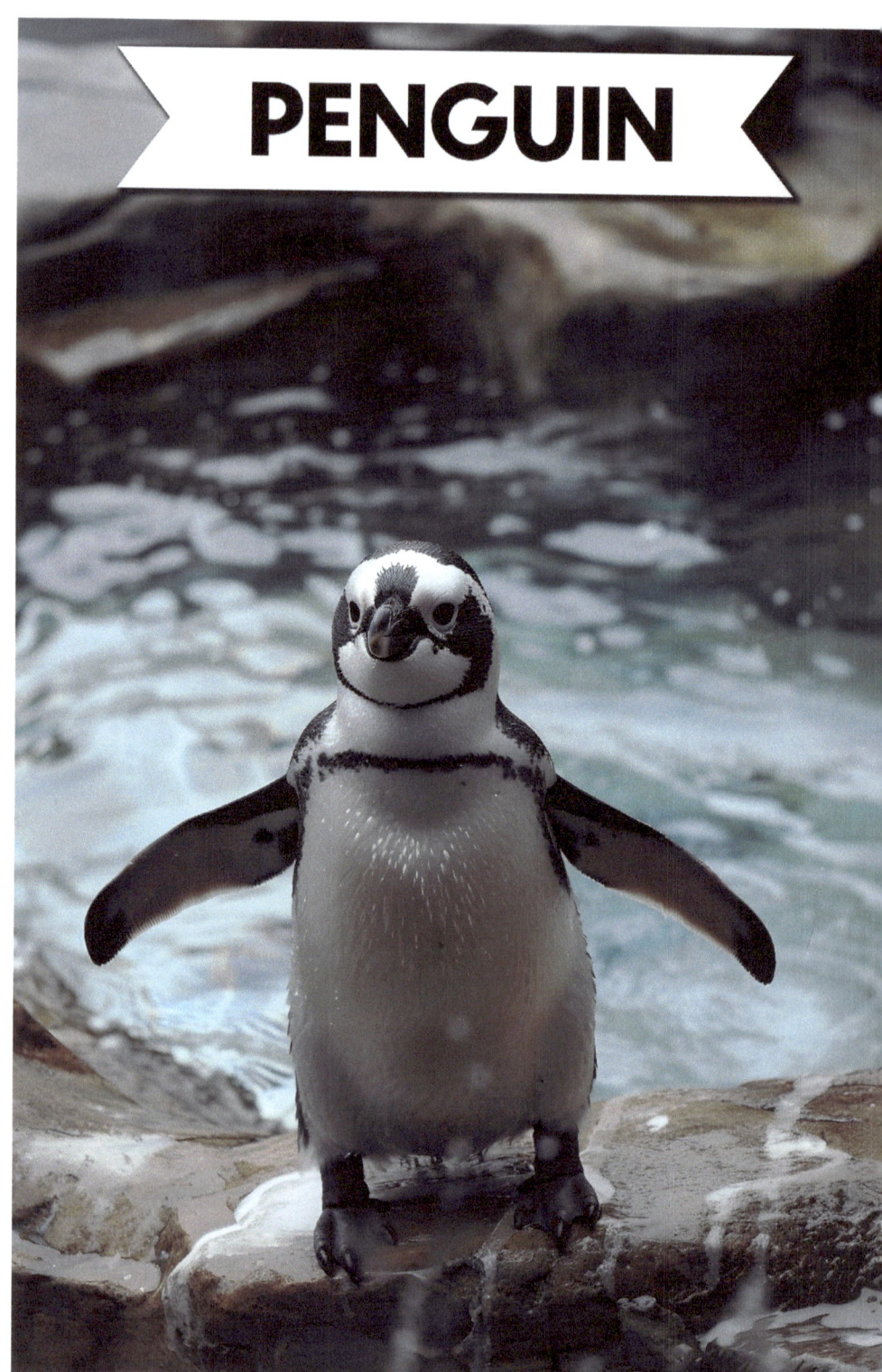

PARROT

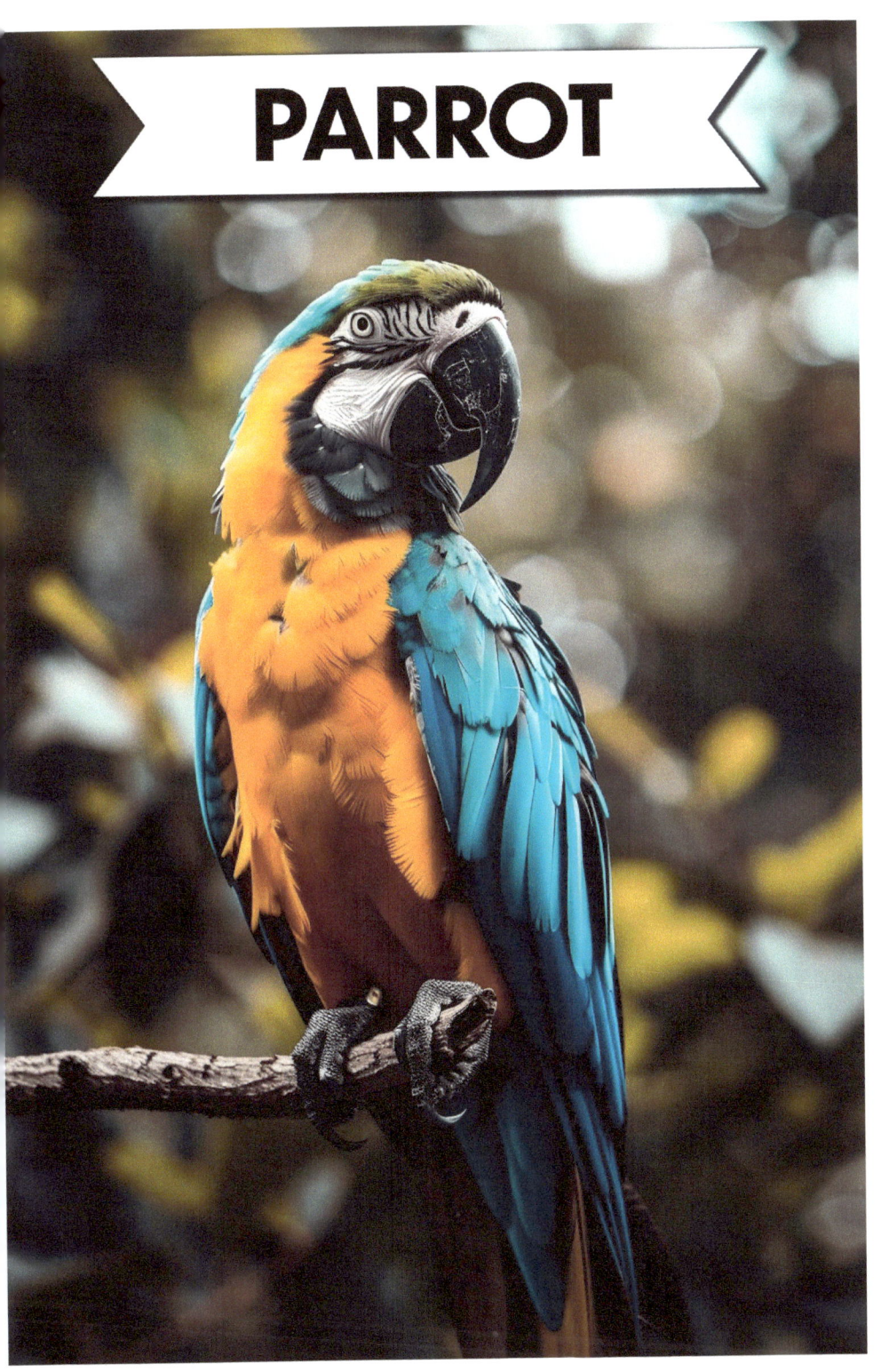

KINGFISHER

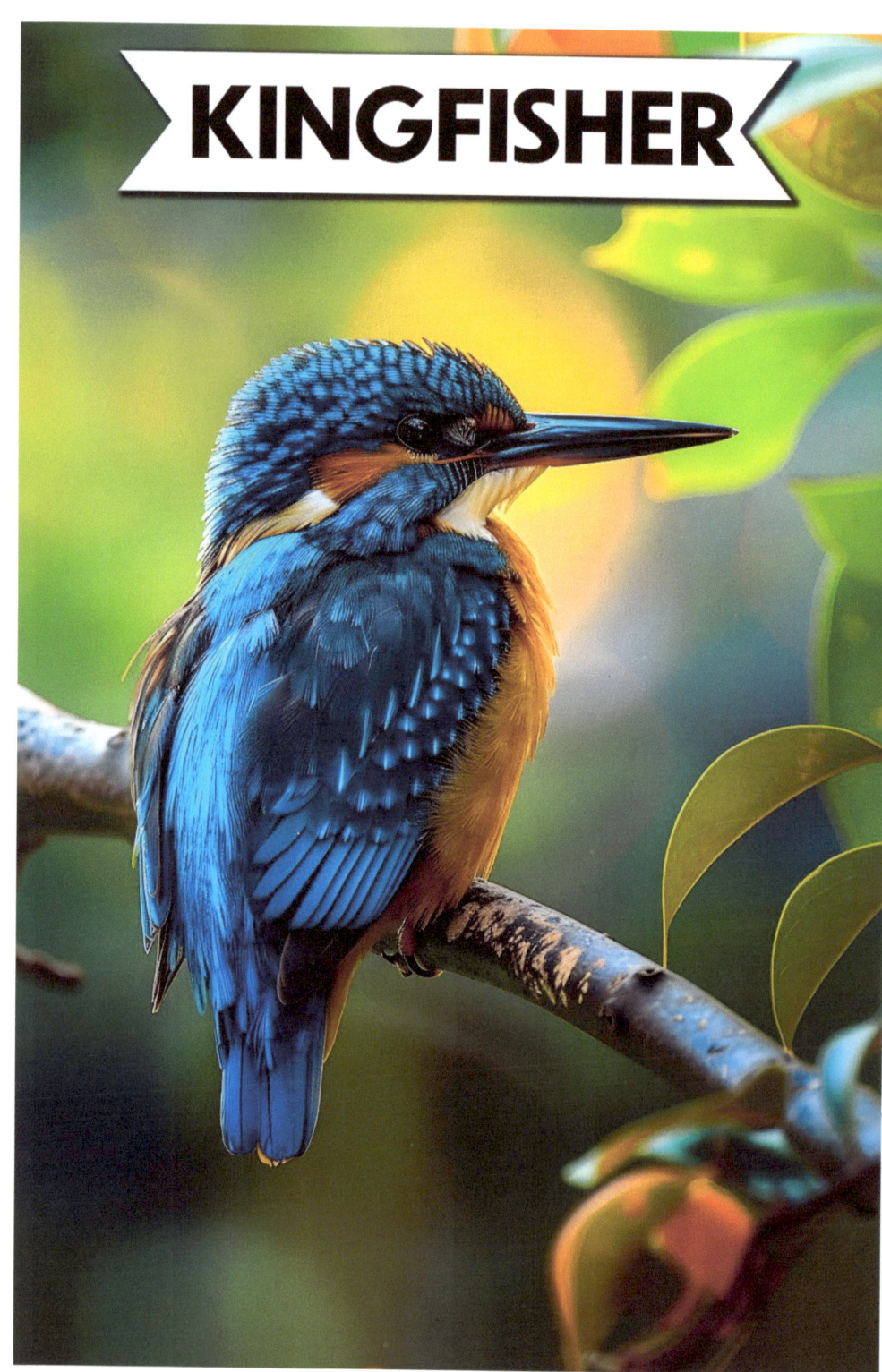

HERON

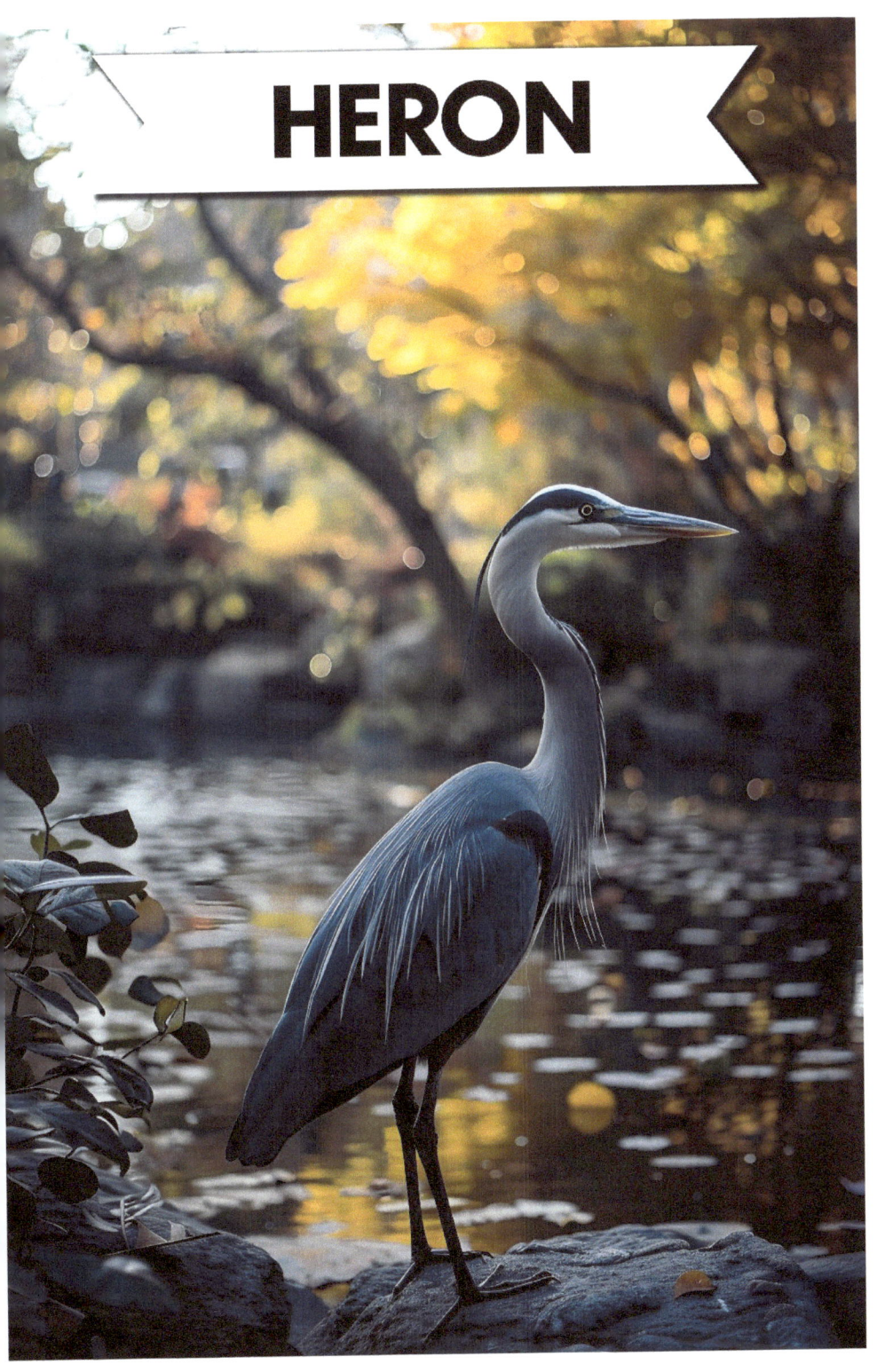

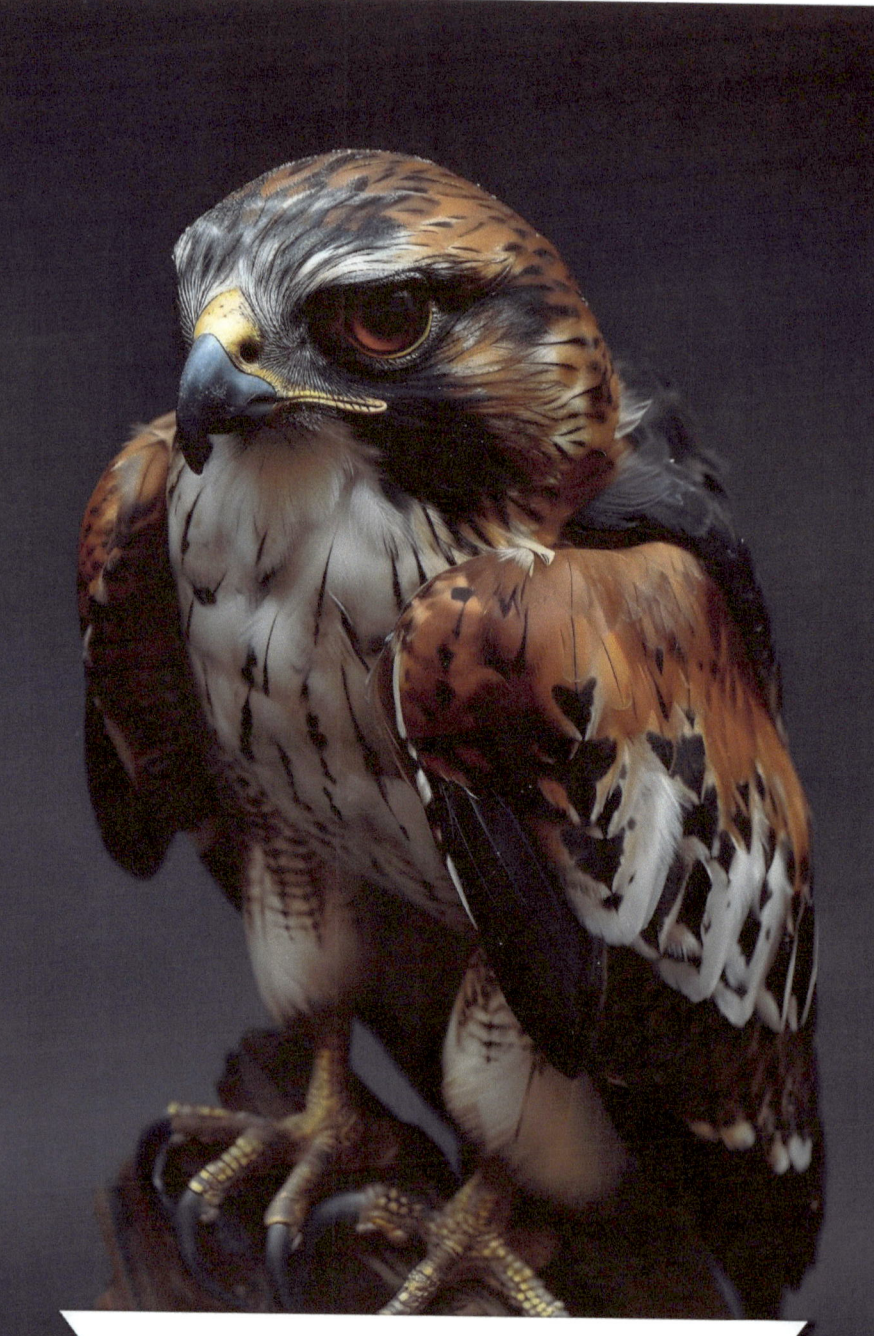

HAWK

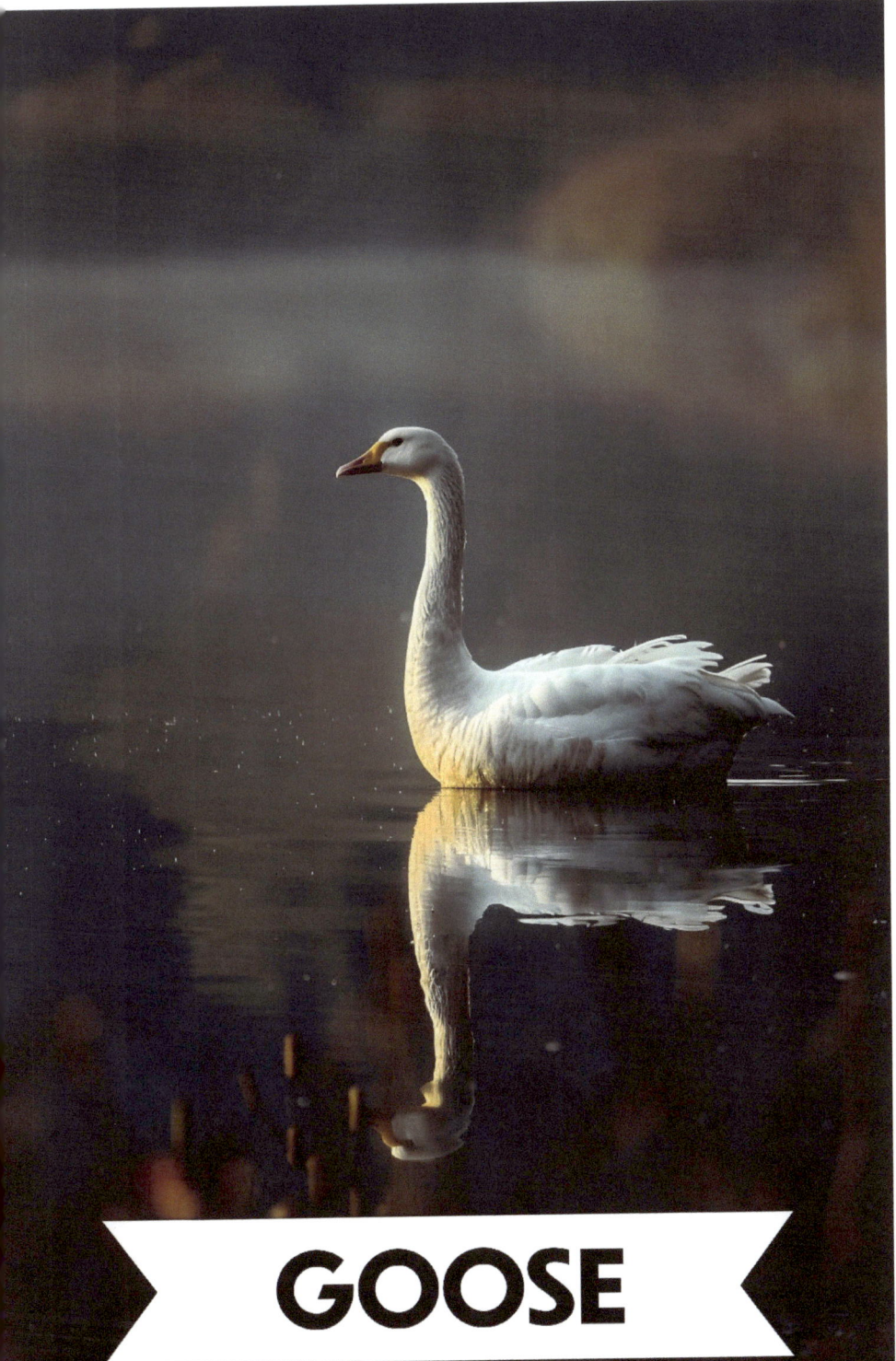

GOOSE

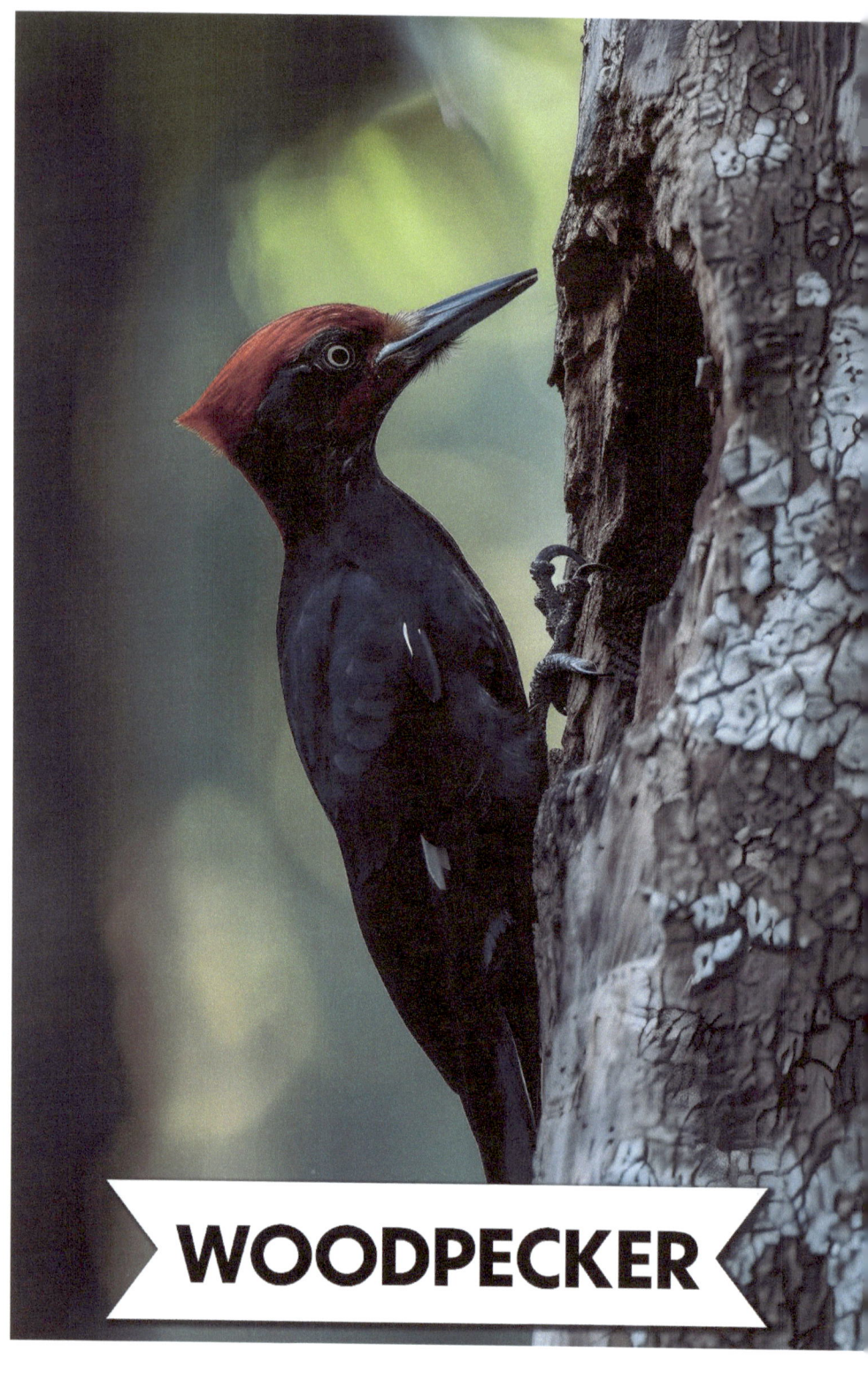

WOODPECKER

TOUCAN

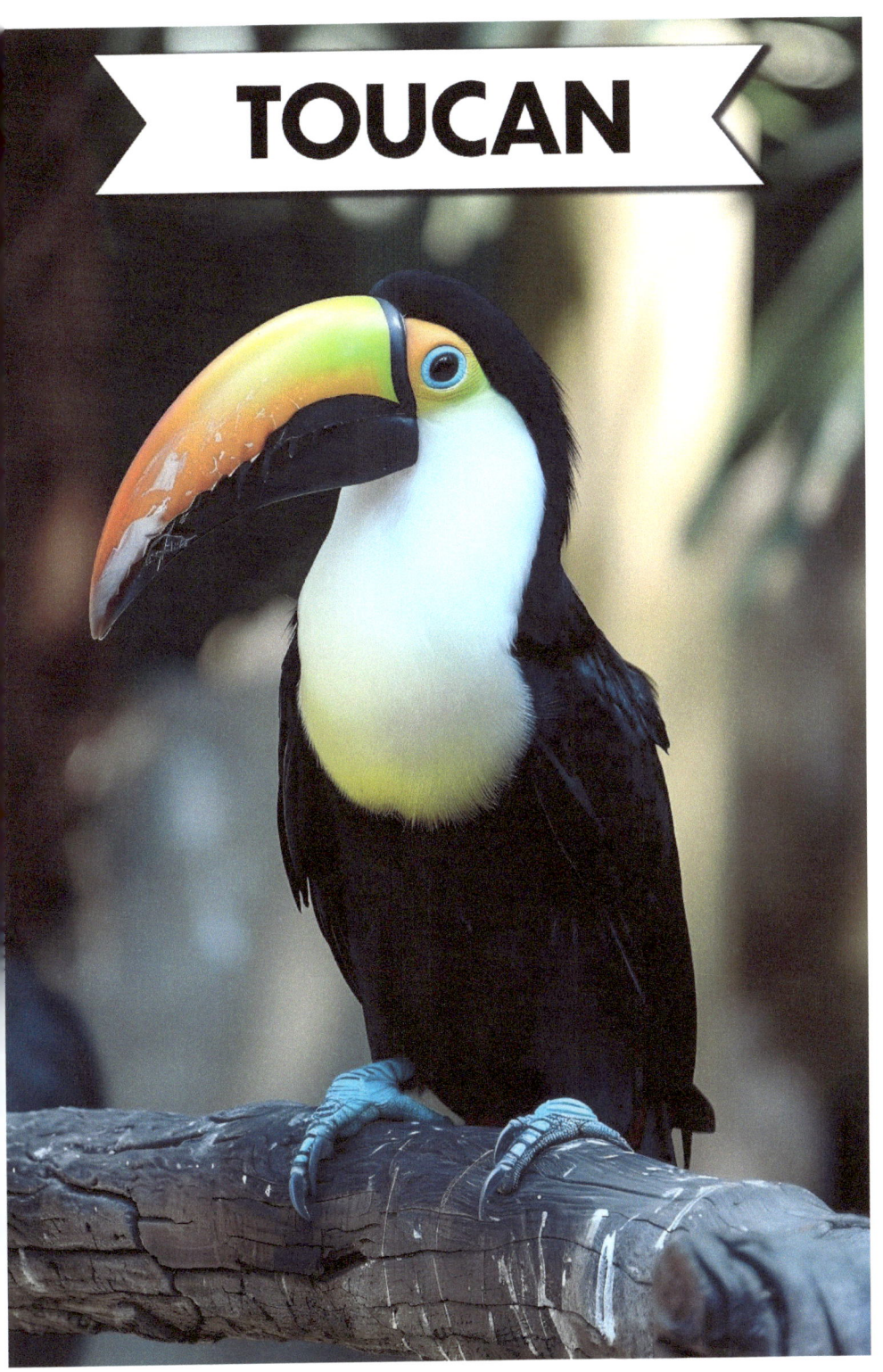

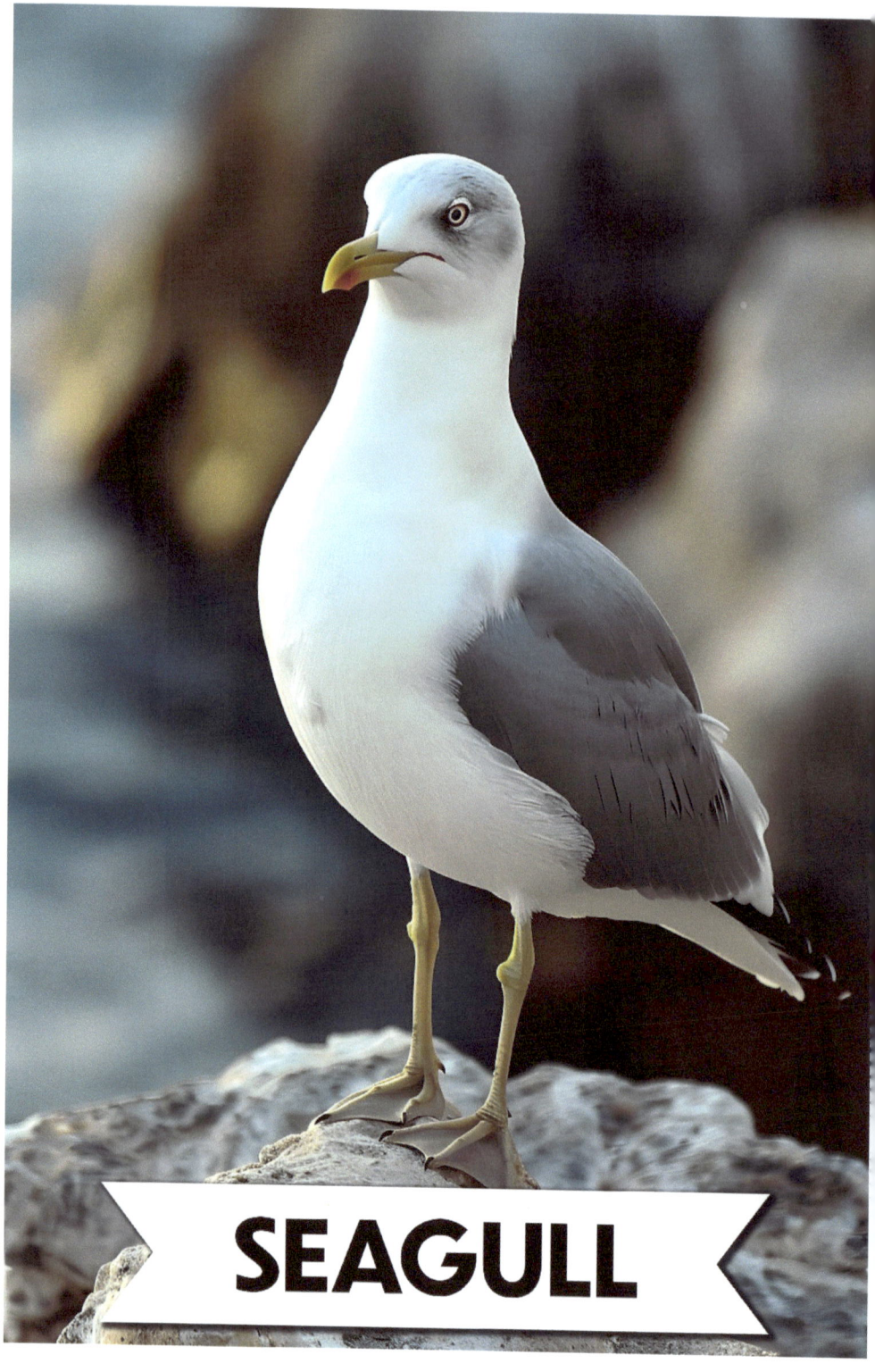

SEAGULL

QUAIL

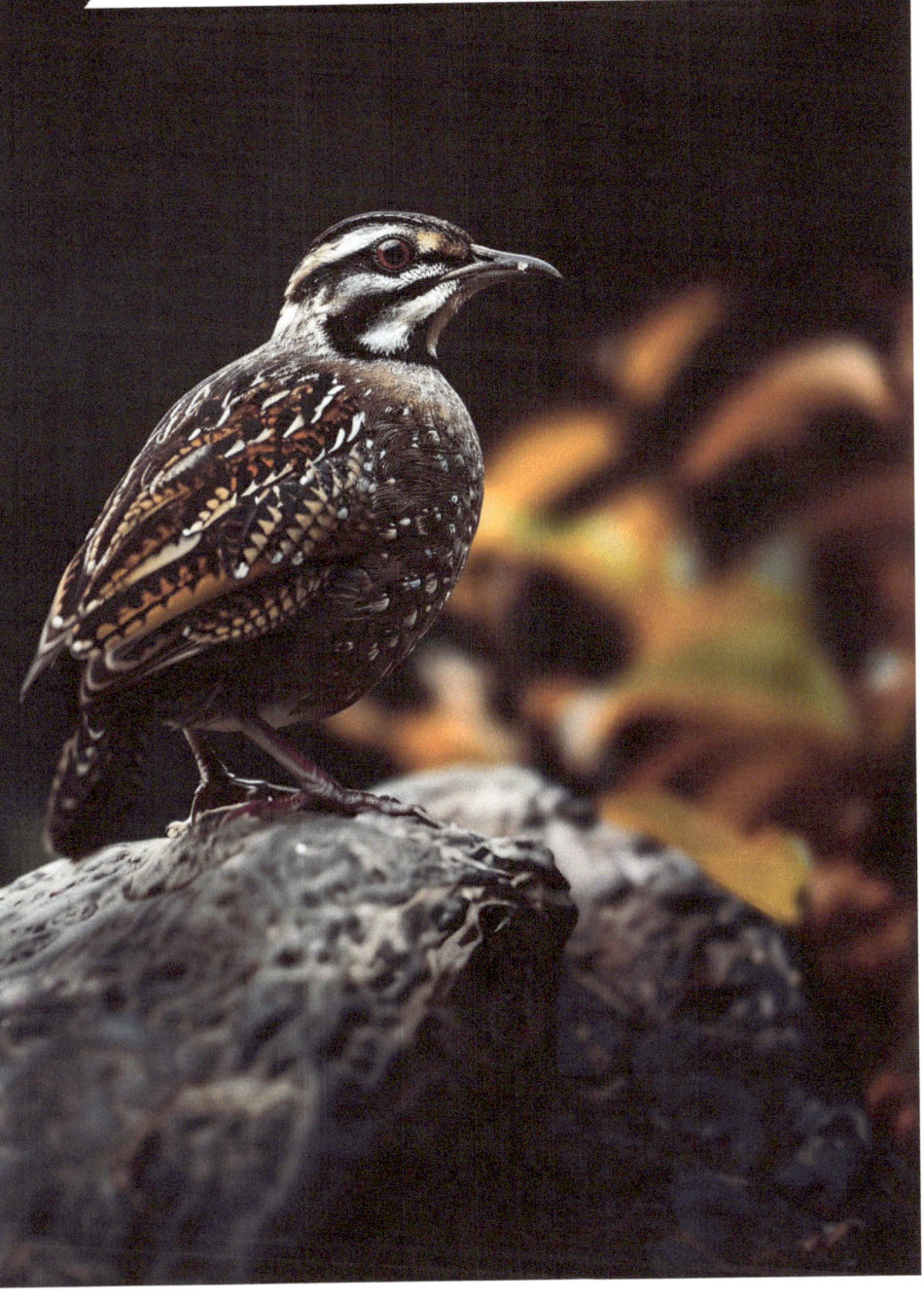

PUFFIN

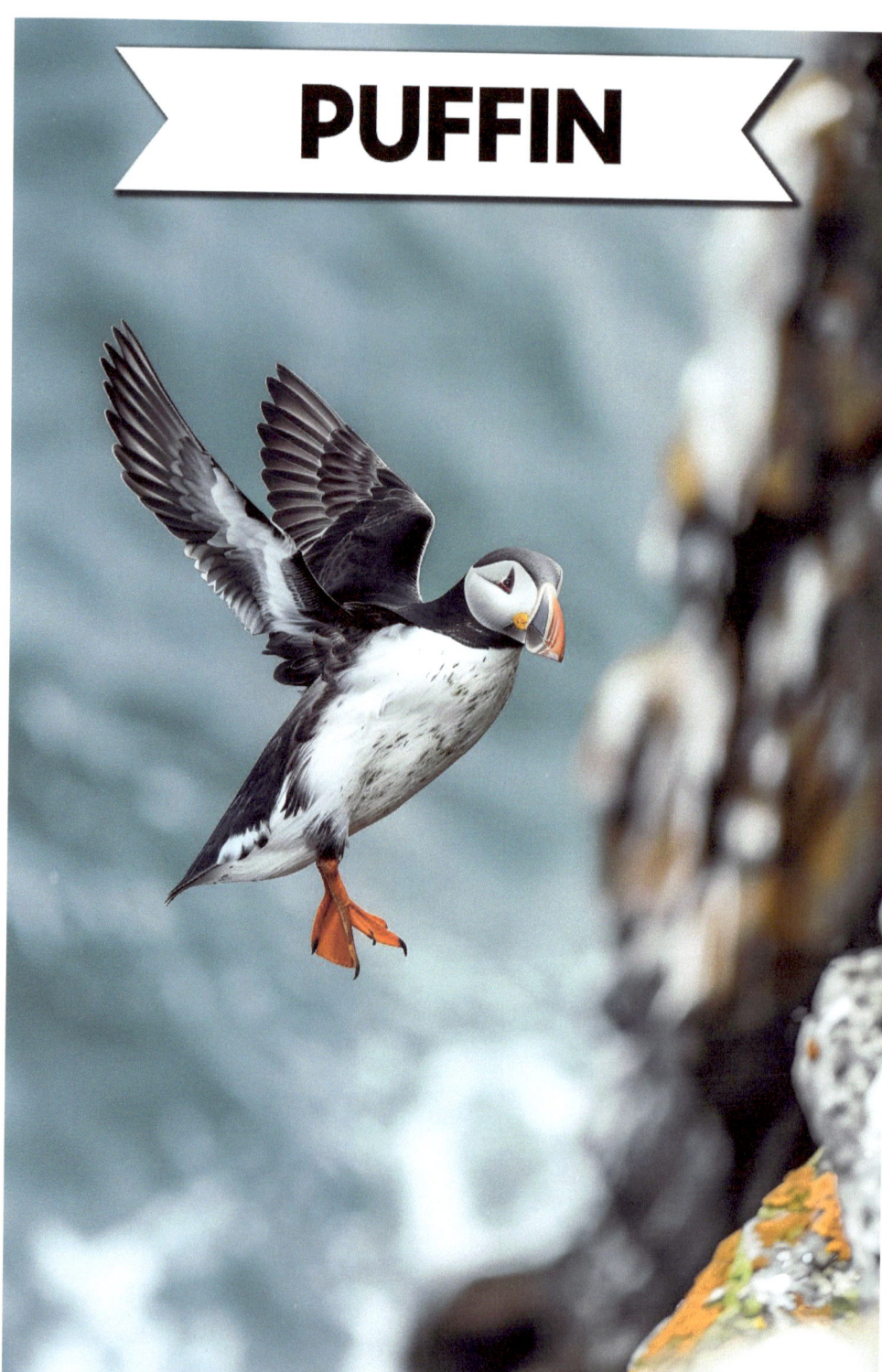

LOVEBIRD

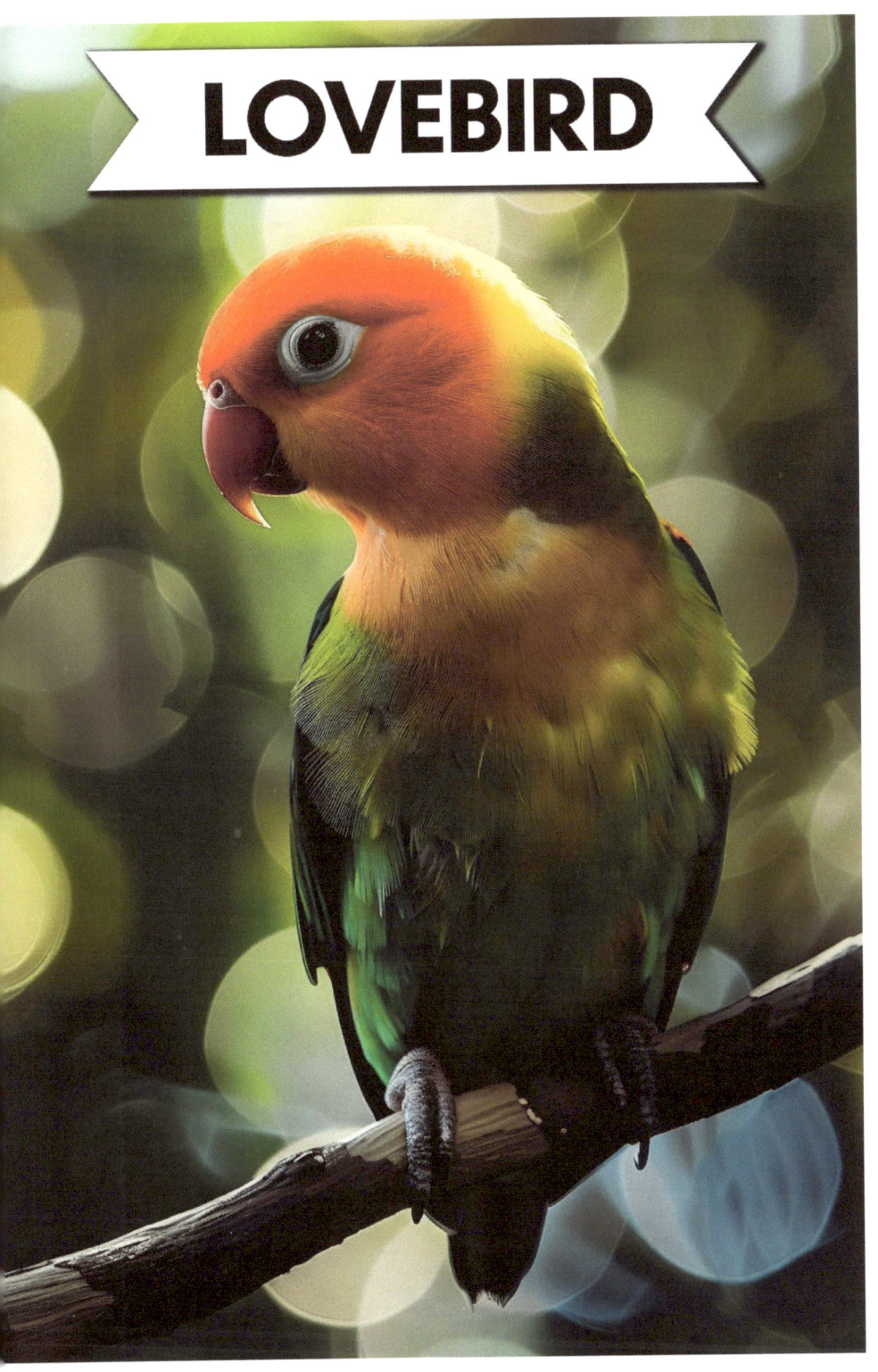

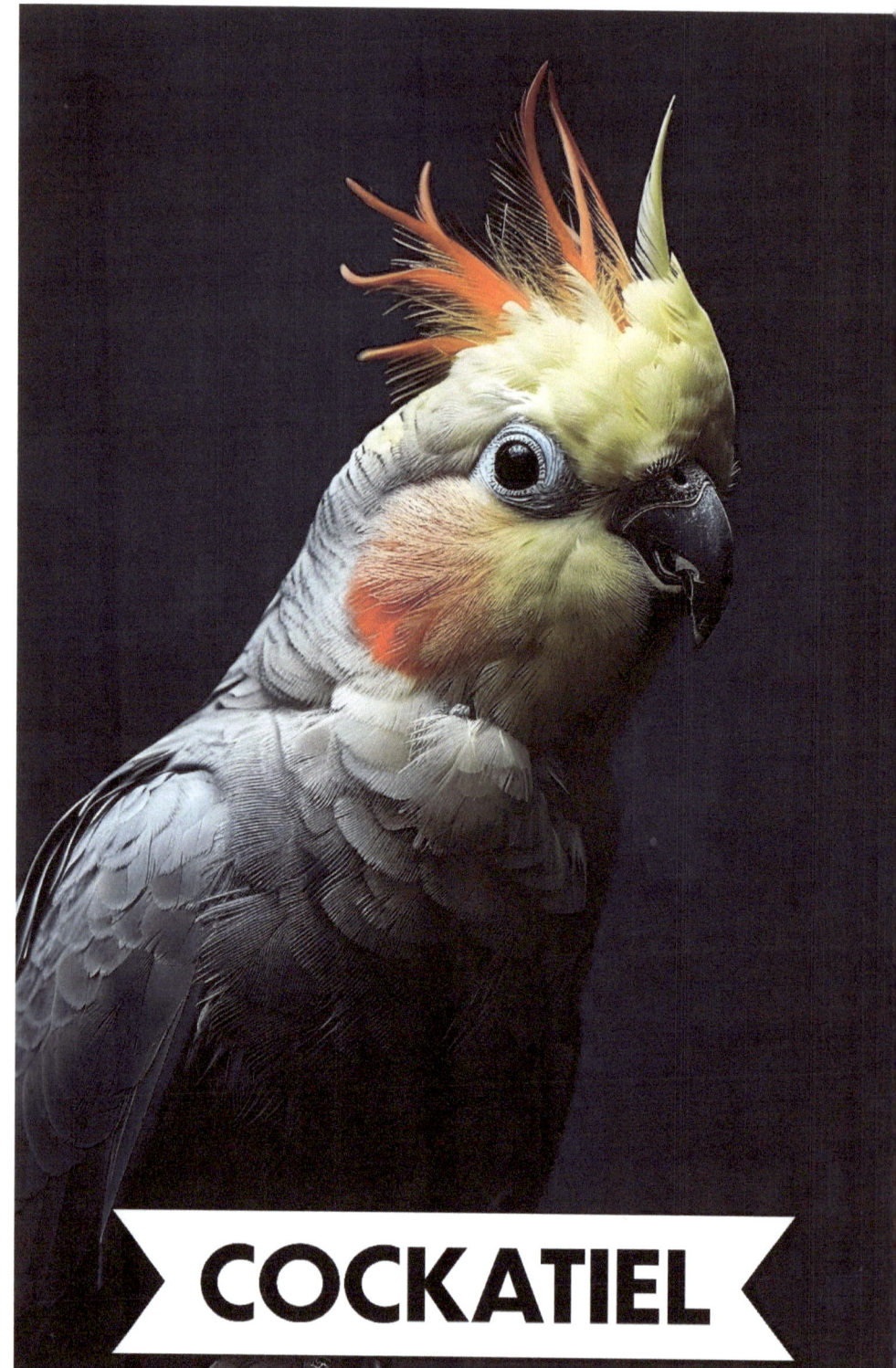

COCKATIEL

MYNA

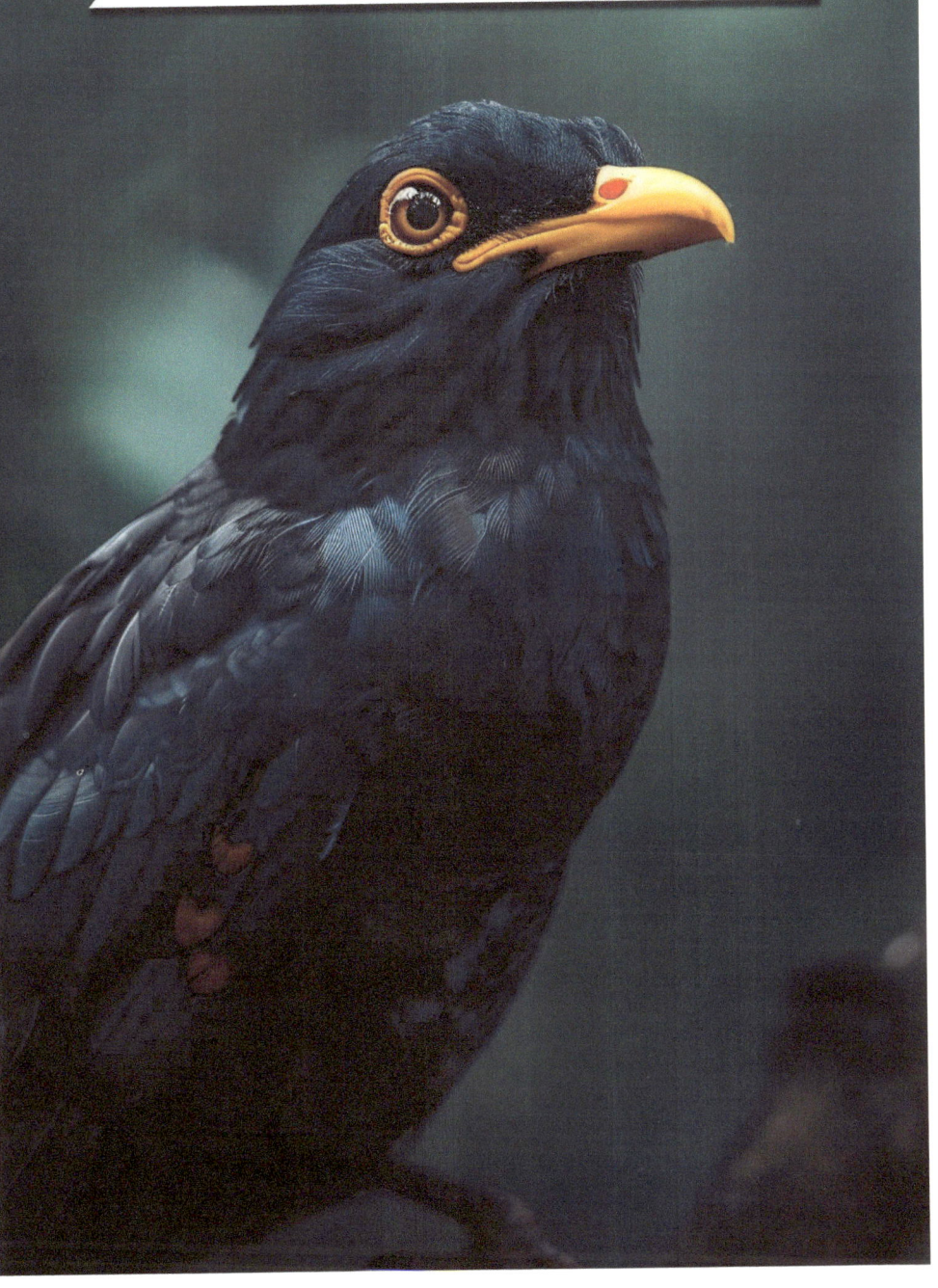

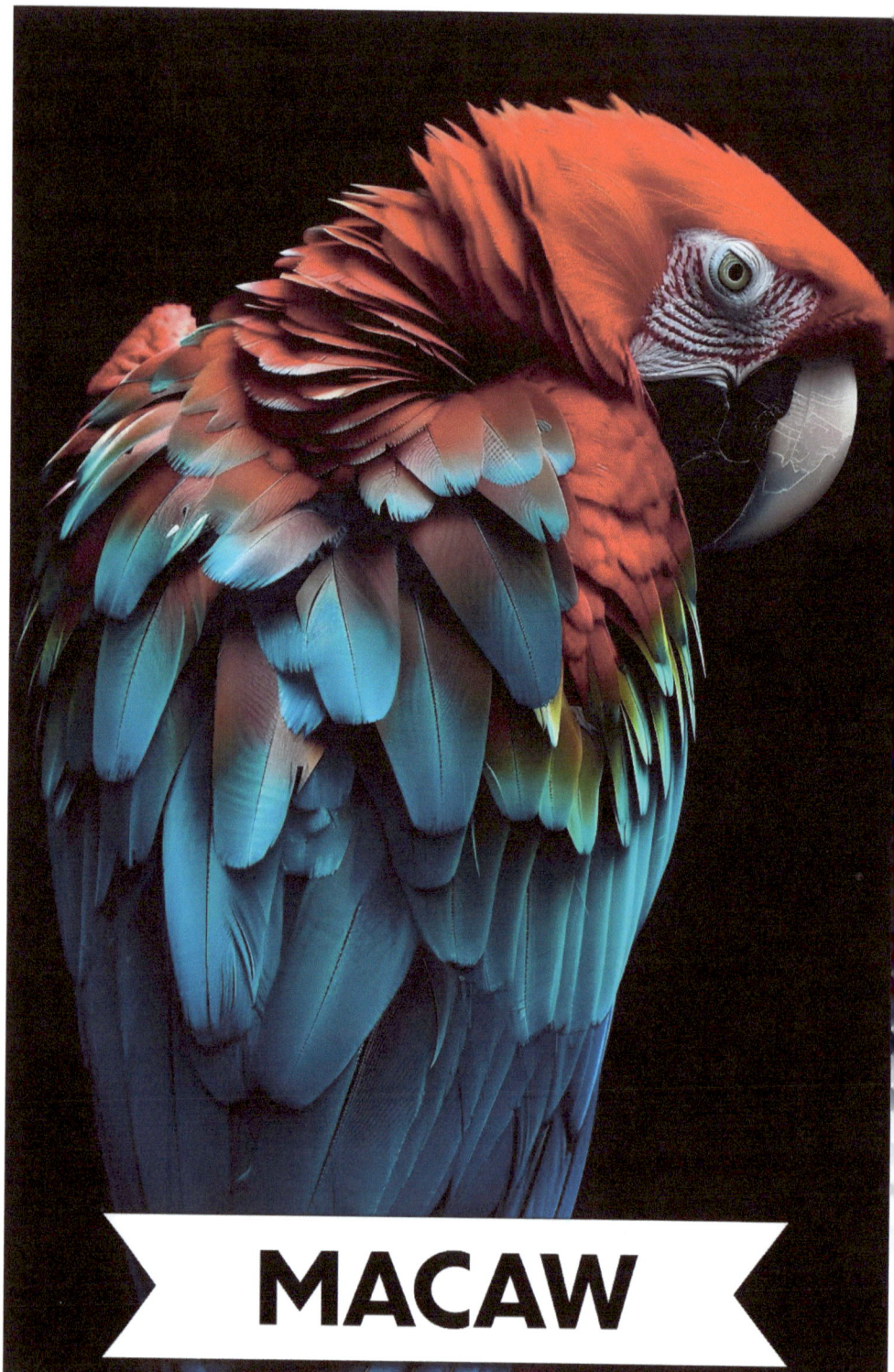

MACAW

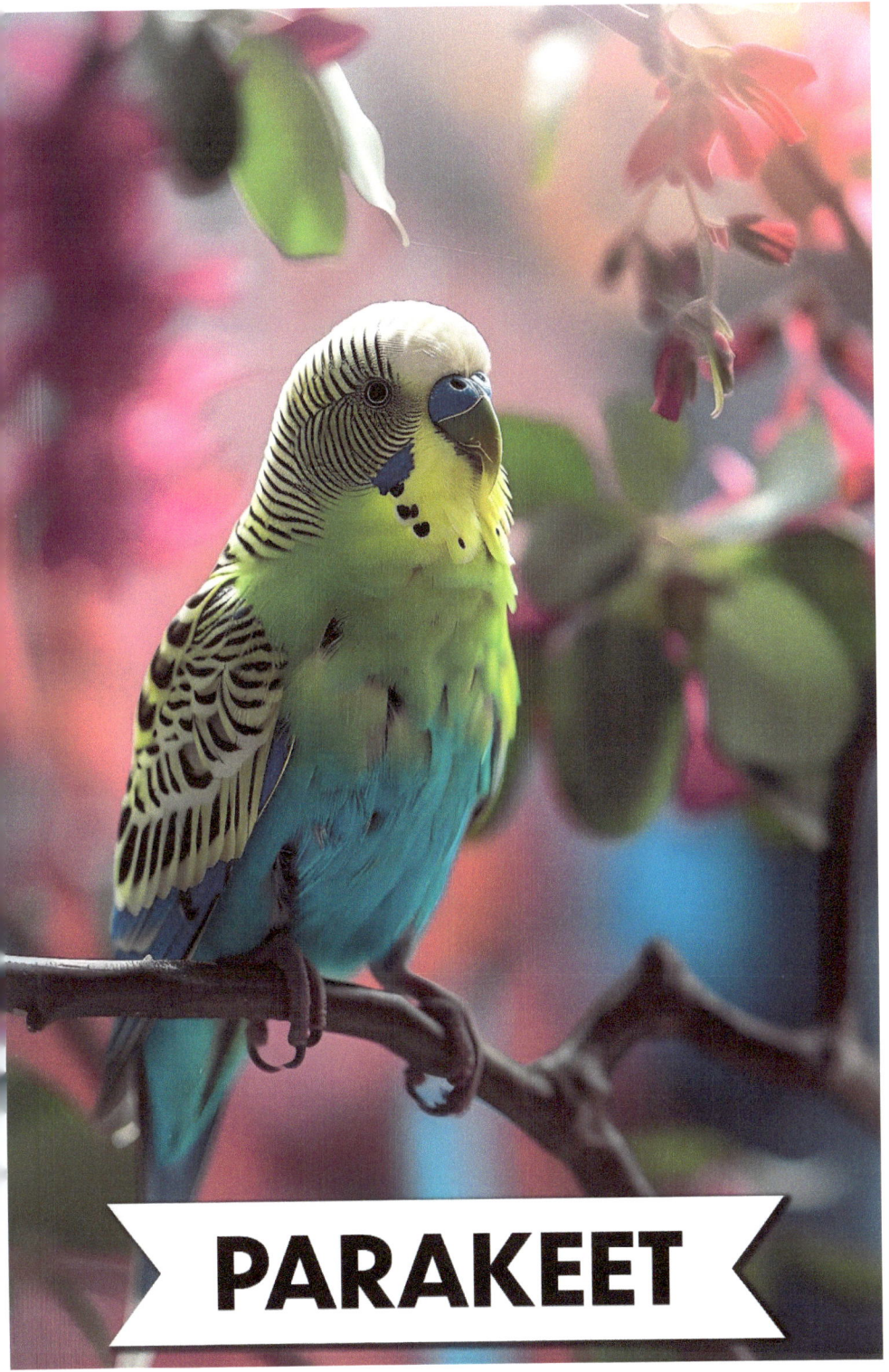

PARAKEET

ORIOLE

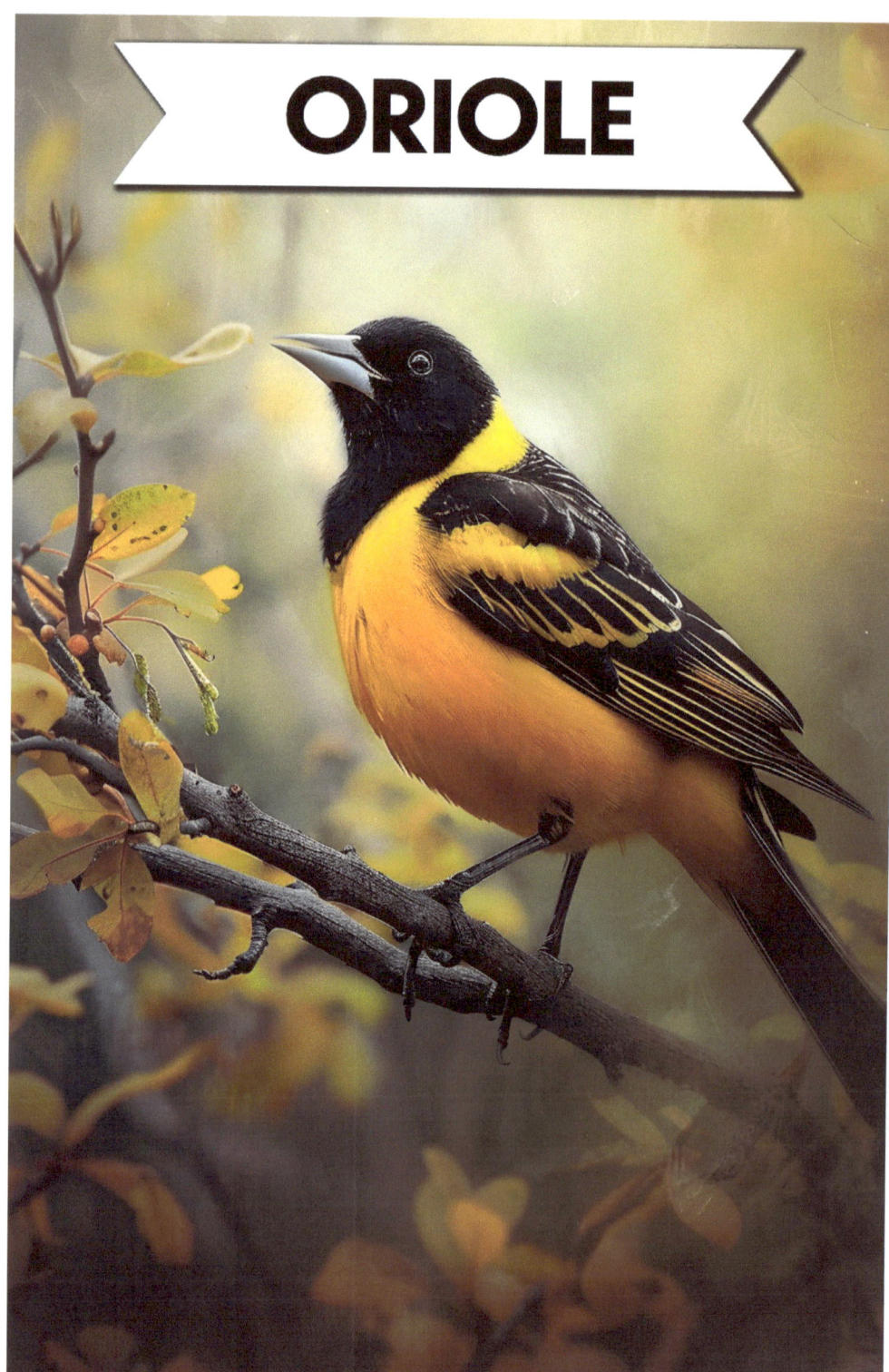

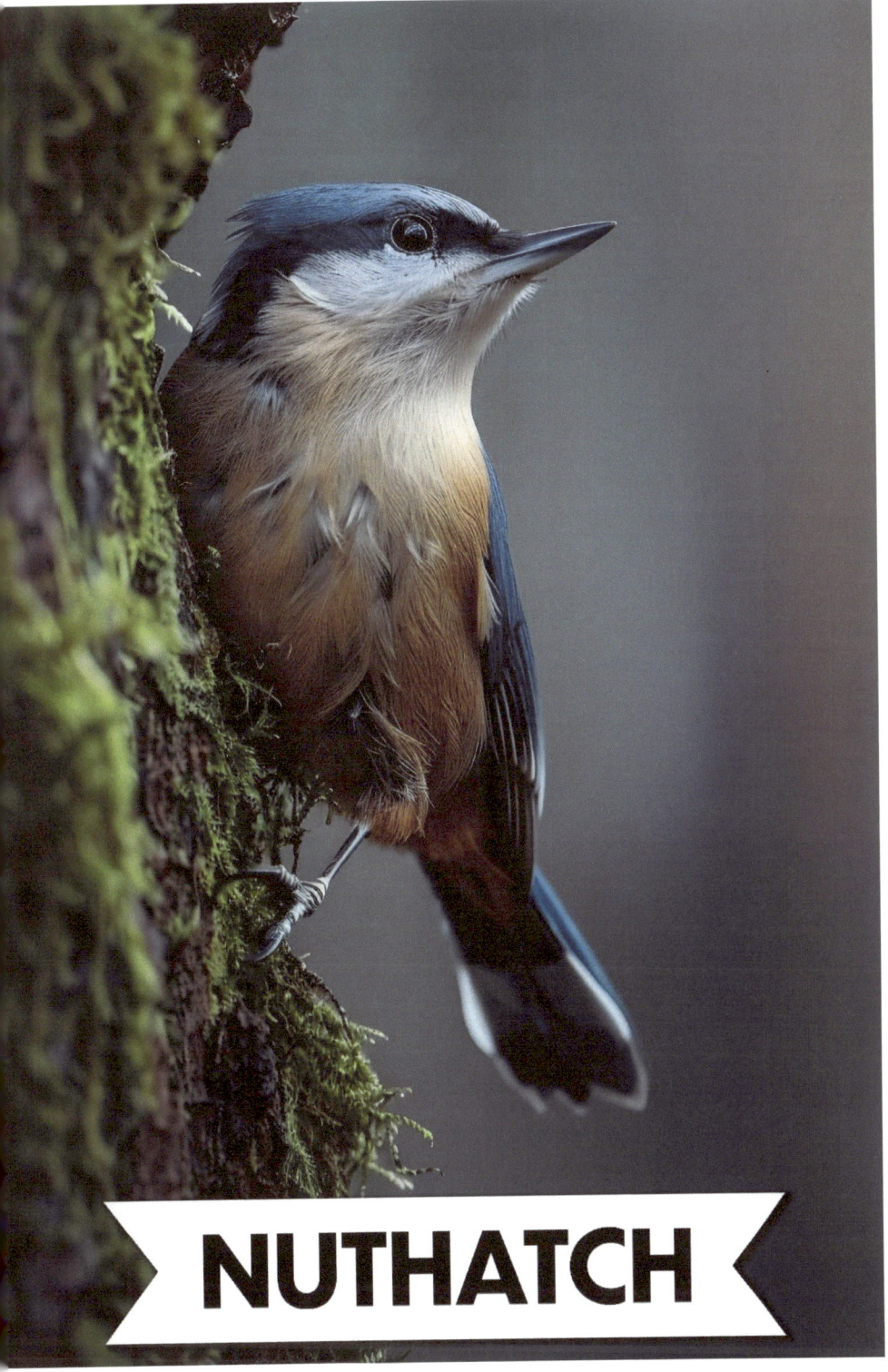

NUTHATCH

SHRIKE

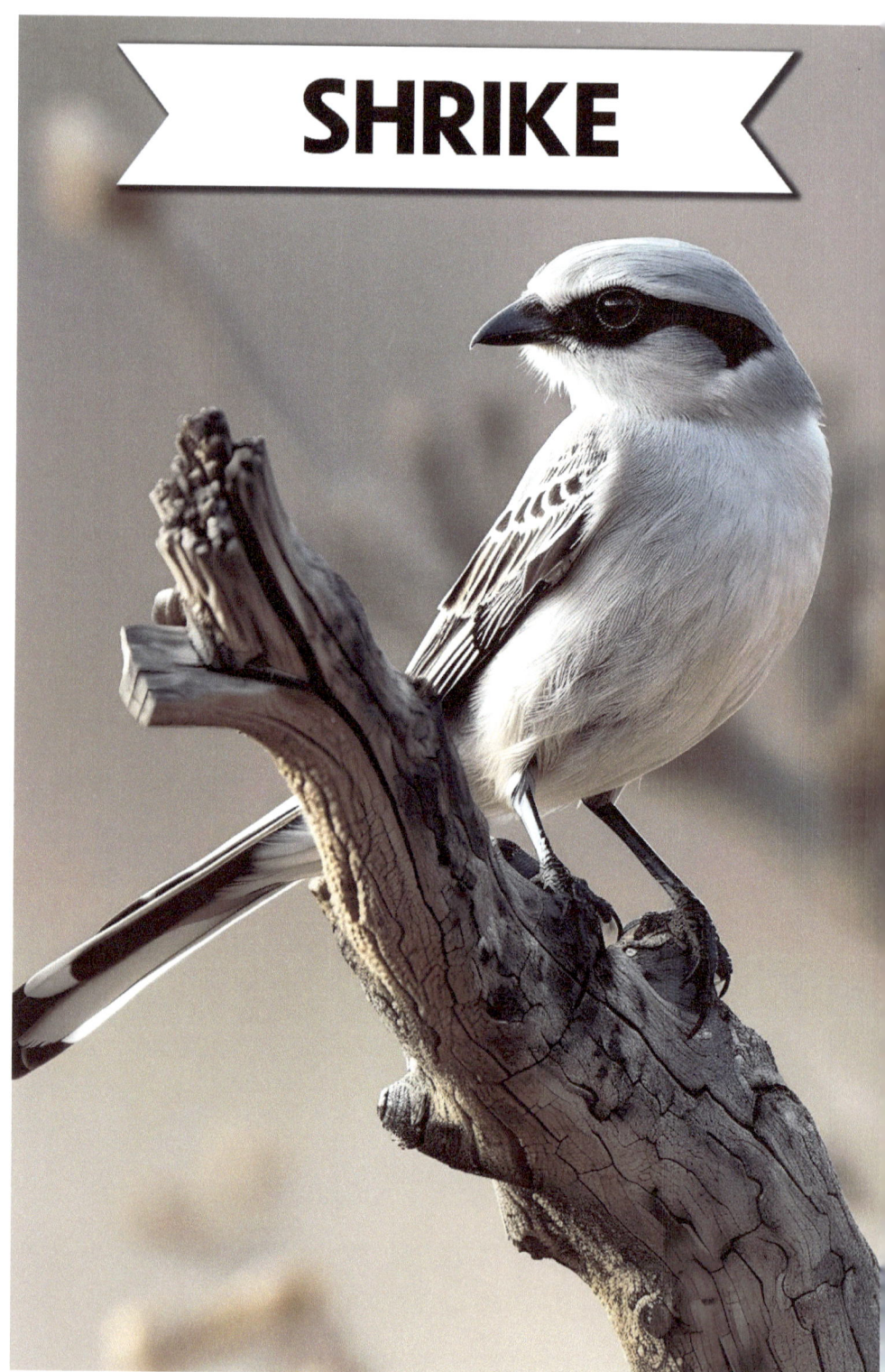

WREN

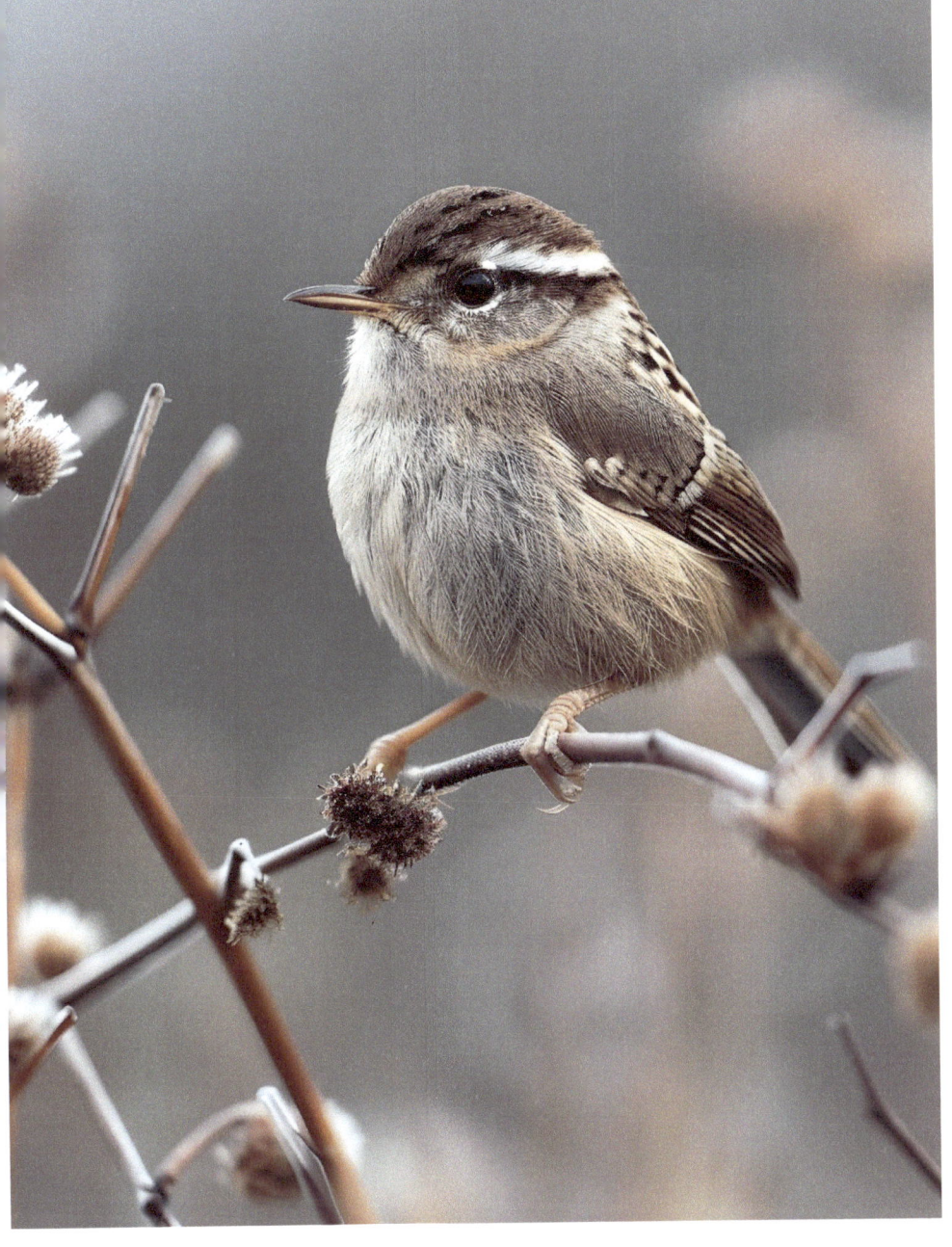

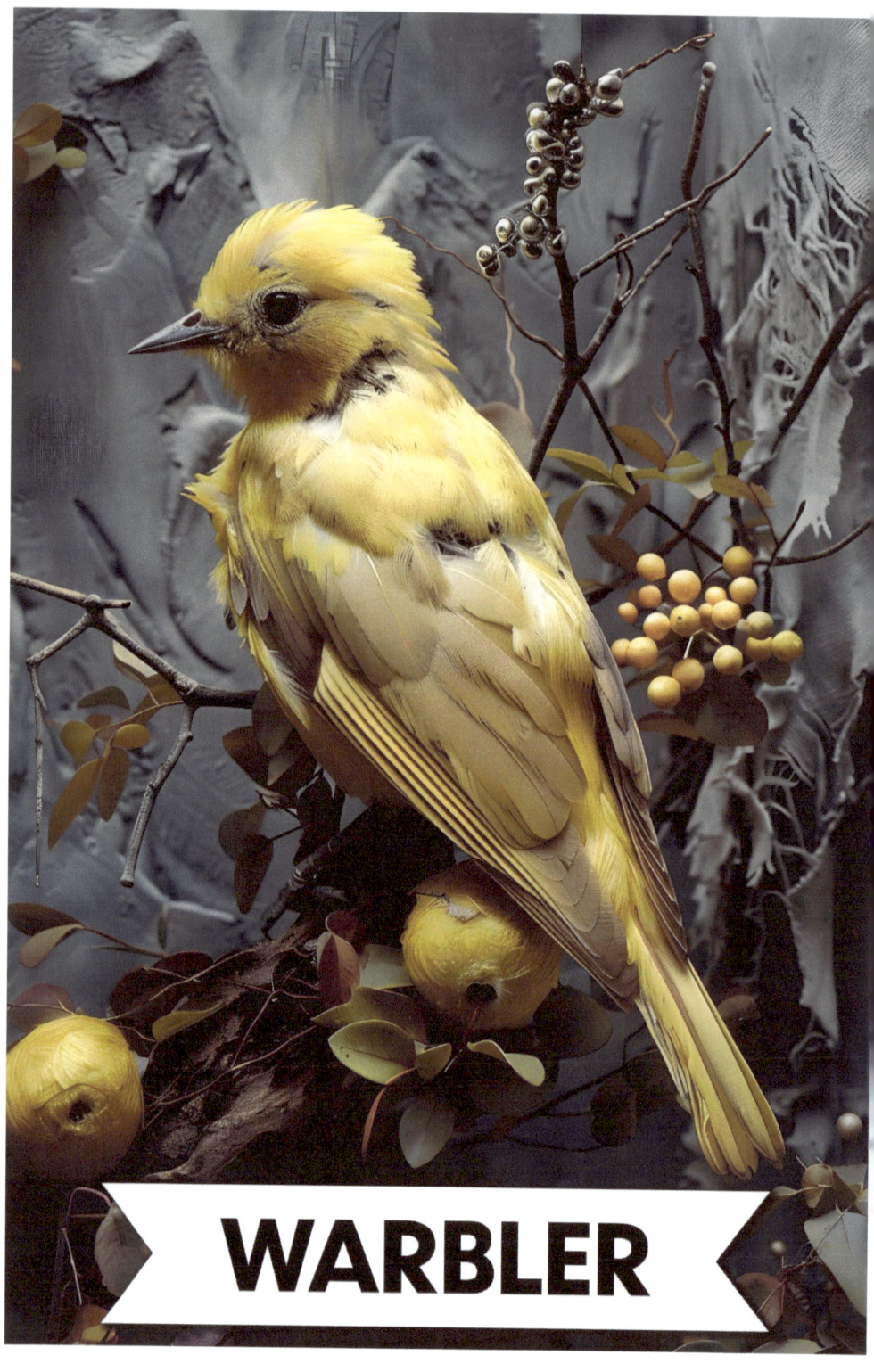

WARBLER

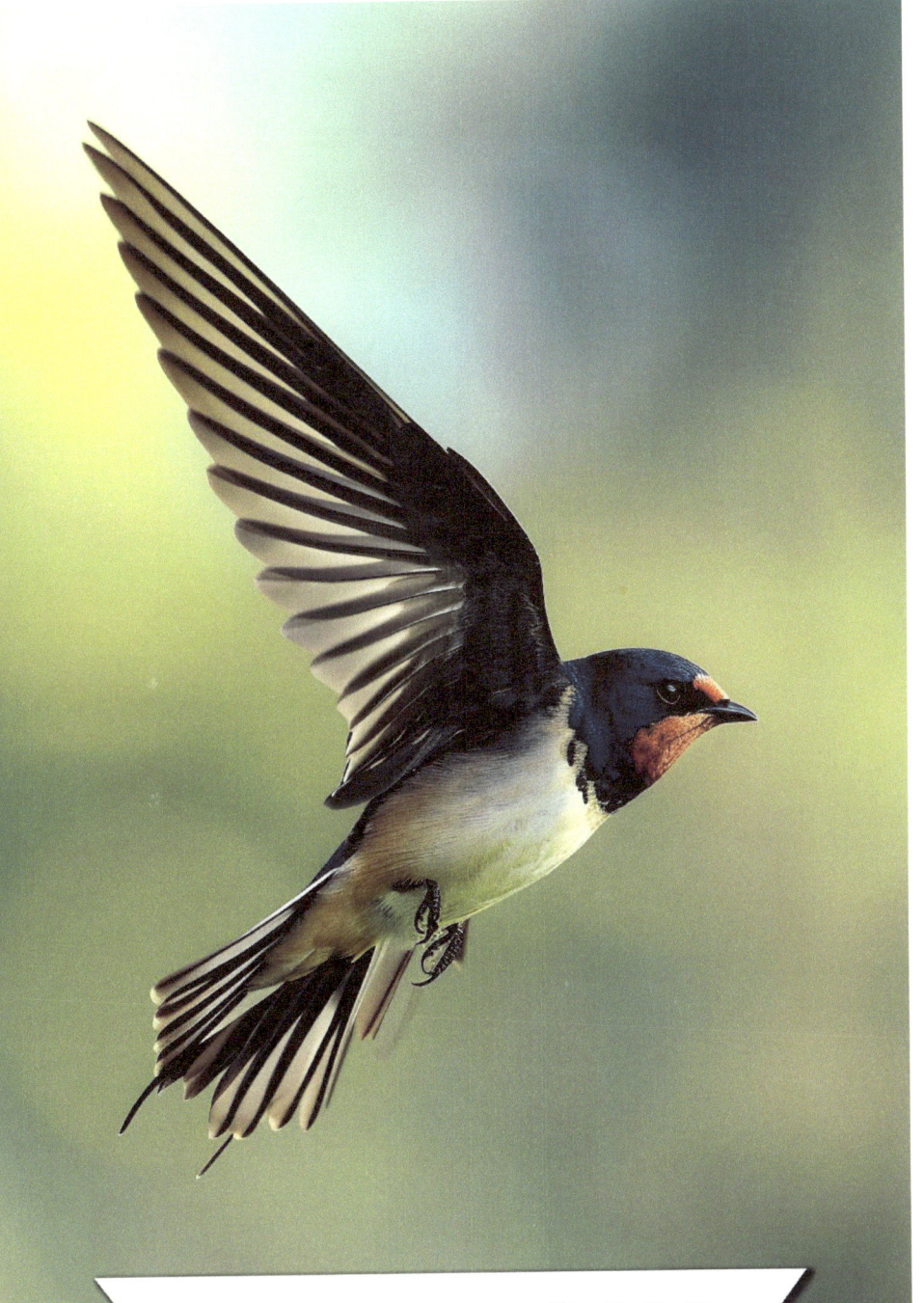

SWALLOW

SPARROW

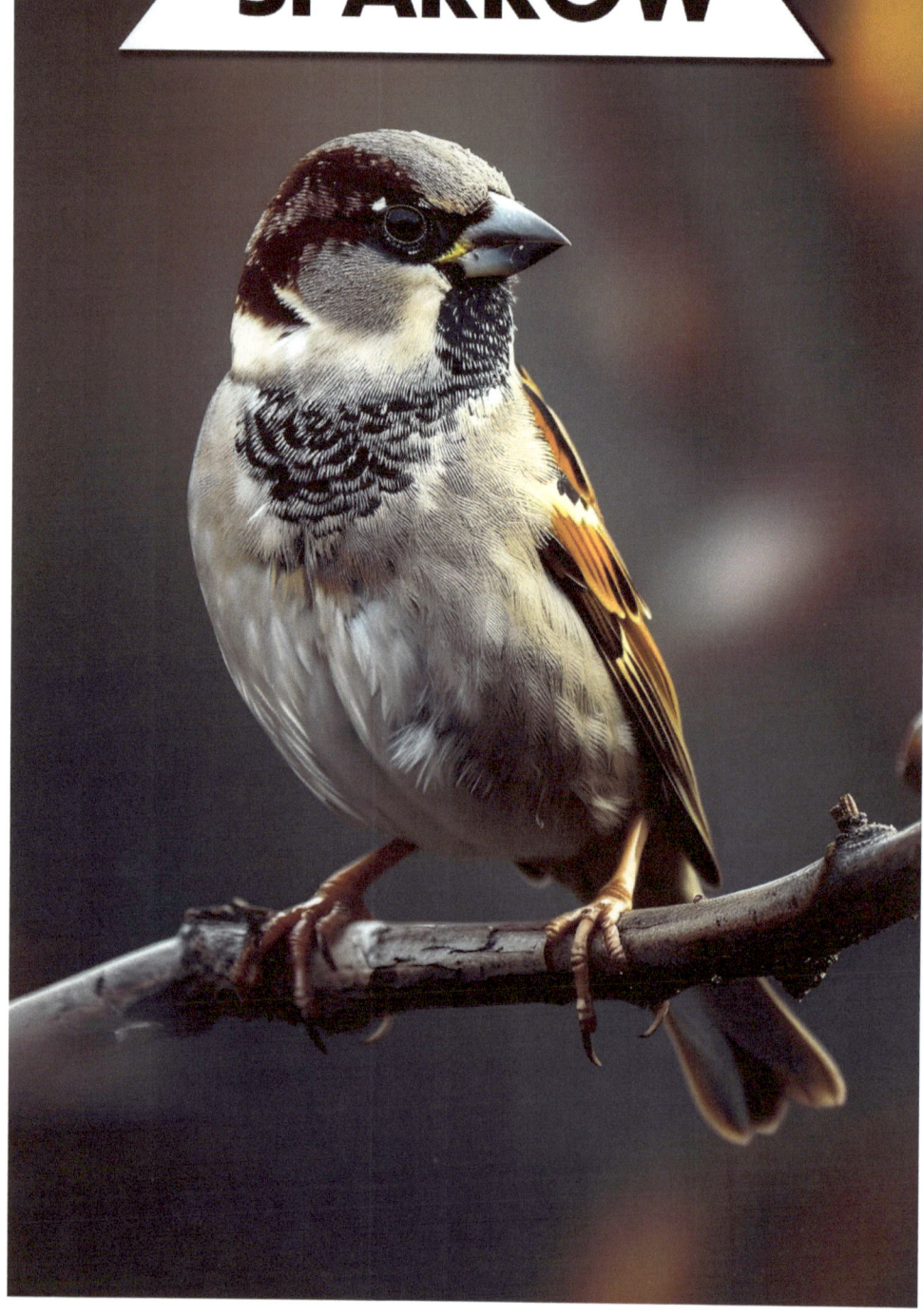